INTERESTS IN ABORTION

With love and thanks to Sean, Luke, Liz and Zac who each in their own way has taught me about what is important in life.

Interests in Abortion
A new perspective on foetal potential and the abortion debate

TRACIE MARTIN
Centre for Human Bioethics
Monash University

Ashgate
Aldershot • Brookfield USA • Singapore • Sydney

© Tracie Martin 2000

All rights reserved. No part of this publication may be reproduced, stored in a retrieval system, or transmitted in any form or by any means, electronic, mechanical, photocopying, recording or otherwise without the prior permission of the publisher.

Published by
Ashgate Publishing Ltd
Gower House
Croft Road
Aldershot
Hants GU11 3HR
England

Ashgate Publishing Company
Old Post Road
Brookfield
Vermont 05036
USA

Ashgate website: http://www.ashgate.com

British Library Cataloguing in Publication Data
Martin, Tracie
   Interests in abortion : a new perspective on foetal potential and the abortion debate. - (Avebury series in philosophy)
   1. Abortion - Moral and ethical aspects 2. Fetus - Legal status, laws, etc. 3. Fetus - Physiology 4. Right to life
   I. Title
   179.76

Library of Congress Catalog Card Number: 99-75546

ISBN 0 7546 1146 9

Printed in Great Britain by
Antony Rowe Ltd, Chippenham, Wiltshire

Contents

Foreword vii
Acknowledgments ix

1 Introduction 1

2 Potential and Physical Dependence 7
    Types of Potential 7
    Foetal Potential 12

3 Foetal Physiology and Active Potential 19
    The Necessary Properties 19
    Physical Foetal Development 23

4 Active Potential and Foetal Psychology 33
    Foetal Learning 37
    A Potential Person 45

5 Personal Identity and the Human Foetus 47
    Parfit's Identity Criterion 47
    Relation R and the Human Foetus 50
    The Potentiality Principle and the Human Foetus 59

6 Potential Persons and Interests 63
    The Right to Continued Existence 63
    Objective and Subjective Interests 64
    Brain Damaged People and Frankenstein 69
    The Post-24-Week-Old Foetus's Right to Continued Existence 70

7 Moral Asymmetry 73
    The Principle of Moral Symmetry 73
    An Asymmetrical Application of the Principle of Moral Symmetry 76

Tooley's Kittens	77
8 The Practical Consequences	**83**
The Case So Far	83
Practicalities and Human Embryos	85
Practicalities and Pre-24-Week-Old Human Foetuses	86
Practicalities and Post-24-Week-Old Human Foetuses	91
Practicalities and Mothers	93
Practicalities and Abnormal Foetuses	96
Practicalities and Non-Human Animals	97
9 Conclusion	**99**
Bibliography	*103*
Index	*109*

Foreword

Killing a person against her will is clearly wrong. But are human foetuses persons, or even potential persons who possess a "right to life"?

Until the 1960s, abortion was not a prominent public issue. In all but a few exceptional circumstances, the procurement of an abortion constituted a criminal offense. Since then many countries have relaxed the prohibition on abortion, or decriminalised the practice. But the debate surrounding the permissibility of some or all abortions is continuing.

Abortion is a moral problem. Very roughly, three different moral positions on abortion are discernible. These can be described as conservative, liberal and moderate. On the conservative view, abortion (from the moment of conception onwards) is almost always seriously wrong; the liberal position holds that abortion is almost never wrong, or if wrong not seriously so; and moderates think that a number of factors (for example, foetal abnormality, maternal health, gestational age) bear on the rightness or wrongness of abortion. Can the moral impasse between these positions be resolved?

Ever since Michael Tooley published his ground-breaking article on "Abortion and Infanticide" in 1972, the abortion debate has largely revolved around questions such as the following: "What is a person?"; "What is it that gives persons the right to life?"; "Is it wrong to kill potential persons?"; and "When in its development from newly fertilised egg to normal adult, does a human individual become a person with a right to life?"

Tooley's answer is that human individuals do not become persons until some time after birth. Moreover, as merely potential persons, foetuses and infants do not have a right to life and it would not be *directly* wrong to cut short the life of a foetus or a newborn child.

Tooley's liberal position will strike many people as counter-intuitive; the same is, however, true of the conservative position which holds that it is just as wrong to destroy a single-cell embryo as it is to destroy a mature person. Moderates who find either view implausible have, however, found it extremely difficult to provide a plausible and internally consistent defence of their position. This is why the present book takes on a special significance. In *Interests in Abortion: A new perspective on foetal potential and the abortion debate* Tracie Martin defends a novel moderate position that accepts elements from both the liberal and the conservative position.

Following Tooley, Martin understands personhood in terms of psychological states and agrees that early foetuses who lack the relevant mental states are not persons. While this might be seen as a victory for the liberal position, Martin then goes on to provide an empirically-based argument for the view that by 24 weeks gestation foetuses have acquired the relevant characteristics that provide strong grounds for thinking that it is directly wrong to kill such foetuses.

Interests in Abortion: A New Perspective on Foetal Potential and the Abortion Debate provides a fertile mix of sophisticated philosophical argument and an impressive array of empirical evidence for a moderate position on abortion. It provides a challenge to both conservatives and liberals to review their moral position on abortion. More than that. The book also challenges the legal boundaries currently drawn around permissible and impermissible abortions and other practices, such as embryo experimentation.

This is an important book that should be read widely. I have great pleasure in recommending it not only to philosophers and bioethicists, but also to health care professionals and public policy makers.

Helga Kuhse
Centre for Human Bioethics
Monash University
May 1999

Acknowledgments

I would like to thank Associate Professor Helga Kuhse, who was my supervisor during the preparation of my Master of Bioethics thesis that forms the basis of this book. She was a source of much valuable advice and criticism, and the development of my thesis would have been considerably more difficult without her support.

I would also like to thank Professor Michael Tooley, who generously wrote many pages of comments in response to the original thesis. I have endeavoured to respond to Professor Tooley's comments during the preparation of this book, and though there are inevitably points of contention that remain between our respective points of view, the version presented here is better as a result of Professor Tooley's criticisms.

I would like to acknowledge the numerous hours that I spent as a student of Dr Justin Oakley. I have learnt a great deal from him, and this book would not have been possible without those hours. Finally, I have also been assisted by conversations with Dr Stephen Buckle, Professor John Bigalow, and Dr Robert Wolfgramm. Each of these people has been a source of advice and assistance, and I am indebted to them for their time.

1 Introduction

Advancing a moderate position on abortion can be likened to opening oneself to attack on all fronts. Those theorists who hold a conservative view on abortion may respond to a moderate position by claiming that a human foetus has a right to continued existence from the moment of conception, or at least from the point of individuation onwards; and that the killing of any human foetus is therefore intrinsically wrong. Such a line of argument often rests on the claim that there is a continuum of foetal development, such that selecting a point along that continuum as a marker of moral standing is merely to make an arbitrary, and thus unjustifiable distinction. Conversely, those theorists who hold a liberal view on abortion may respond to a moderate position by claiming that there is no justifiable basis with which to grant a right to continued existence to a foetus at any stage of its development. And, that without such a right there can be no intrinsic wrongness associated with the killing of a foetus no matter how far advanced the pregnancy may be. Such an argument may well rest on the claim that a right to continued existence is a result of a being's self-awareness, and that as no human foetus is self-aware no human foetus has a right to continued existence that is overridden if it is aborted. Furthermore, some feminist theorists would continue, even if it were the case that human foetuses did have an interest in continued existence, a woman's right to control what happens in and to her own body is a fundamental human right that ought to take precedence over any rights attributable to the unborn human foetus.[1] In response to claims such as these, the arguments developed within these pages are aimed at providing a philosophically sound justification for a moderate position on abortion.

The position on abortion put forward here will not, however, rest on any of the commonly discussed markers such as foetal quickening or viability, which have been successfully challenged on many previous occasions.[2]

---

[1] See, for example, Judith Jarvis Thompson (1971) 'A Defence of Abortion', pp. 47-66 of *Philosophy and Public Affairs*, 1 (1).
[2] See, for instance, Peter Singer (1993) *Practical Ethics* (2nd Ed), Cambridge University Press, Cambridge.

Rather, the argument will ultimately rest on empirically testable claims concerning the human foetus's psychological development. I will argue that a human foetus's psychological development is such that it gives rise to a morally relevant form of potential prior to the foetus's birth, and that abortion is *prima facie* wrong from the time the foetus possesses such a potential.

Underlying this claim is the belief that what is important about a being - what is significant in determining how it ought to be treated - is its psychological capacities. As such, the argument presented will, to a large degree, revolve around Tooley's discussion of abortion and potential personhood.[3] It will be argued that whilst Tooley's understanding of personhood is acceptable, it is too narrow to encompass the full range of beings that can possess a right to continued existence. More specifically, I will claim that whilst Tooley is correct to say that a person is definable on the basis of his/her psychological states, his claim that only past or presently exercised psychological states are morally relevant in the ascription of an interest in continued existence is incorrect: the capacity to experience such states in the future is, I will argue, also relevant. This being so, I will go on to show that not only can actual persons possess a right to continued existence, but potential persons: that is, beings which possess an active potential to become persons, can also possess a right to continue to exist. In which case, if it can be shown that human foetuses at some point in their development come to possess an active potential to become persons, it will simultaneously be shown that human foetuses can possess an interest in continued existence. And, if human foetuses, at some point in their development, come to have an interest in continued existence, then the abortion and consequent death of any such foetus is *prima facie* wrong.

To this end, I will begin my discussion by addressing Tooley's claim that no human foetus can have a right to continued existence based on its potential personhood, because no human foetus can have an active

---

[3] It should be noted at this point that the term "personhood" will be used throughout this paper as a moral term, not merely as a term denoting membership of the species Homo Sapien. Michael Tooley (1983) *Abortion and Infanticide*, Clarendon Press, Oxford. Although there are other theorists who hold positions similar to that of Tooley (see Singer, *ibid.* for example), Tooley's discussion of the issues involved in support of the claim that potential personhood is not morally relevant is perhaps the most comprehensively developed.

potential to become a person. If this were so, if Tooley were correct in his claim that the human foetus's potential is not a fully active potential, then the power to become a person would not be found solely within the foetus. And, if additional morally significant external factors were necessary in order for a foetus to become a person, then Tooley would be correct to conclude that there is no basis on which to ascribe a right to continued existence to a foetus. It is my belief, however, that Tooley is incorrect in this. It will be argued in the next chapter that any physiological dependencies a human foetus has may also be present in actual persons in some instances, and that the presence of these dependencies does not alter an actual person's moral status. So long as a being possesses the psychological capacities definitive of persons, its physiological requirements do not affect its moral standing as a person. The same, I will argue, is true in the case of human foetuses.

The morally relevant causal factors that are necessary for a being to be classified as a potential person are psychological factors; as such they are unaffected by the being's dependence on another for the meeting of its physiological needs. So long as the morally relevant causal factors required for potential personhood are only psychological in nature, and so long as a human foetus has within itself all of the morally relevant factors which are necessary for potential personhood, its physiological dependence on the external world is irrelevant to the determination of its moral status.

Chapters Three and Four will then investigate the possibility that a human foetus possesses all of the morally relevant causal factors that are identified in Chapter Two as necessary for a being to have an active potential to become a person. To this end the physiological and psychological development of the human foetus will be closely examined. It will be argued that on the basis of the information we currently possess concerning a human foetus's development, it appears that a human foetus acquires an active potential to become a person at approximately 24 weeks of development. It will be my contention that the human foetus's potential to become a person is transformed at this time from a previously latent potential to become a person, to an active potential to become a person.

Chapter Five will address the issue of personal identity. For an argument from potential to succeed it must be the case that the potential person and the actual person are the very same being. I will show, in this chapter, that not only does a post-24-week-old human foetus have an active potential to become a person, it also shares at least a weak version of Parfit's Relation R with the person it becomes. I will then argue that a weak version of

Relation R is sufficient for a human foetus to be the very same enduring subject of experiences as the person it becomes. And, that as the foetus and the person it becomes are the very same enduring subject of experiences, the rights of the actual person are attributable to the post-24-week-old foetus. This being so, I will argue, it is *prima facie* wrong to destroy a human foetus from 24 weeks of development onwards. Having made the claim that it is *prima facie* wrong to destroy the post-24-week-old foetus in Chapter Five, I will turn, in Chapter Six, to look more closely at Tooley's claim that only actual persons can possess a right to continued existence. It will be my contention that Tooley has not put forward a convincing case for limiting the right to continued existence to actual persons.

Finally, in Chapter Seven I will discuss Tooley's claim that it can be no more wrong to destroy a potential person, than it is wrong to fail to actualise a possible person. If Tooley were correct in this claim, it would follow that one could not coherently assert that it was wrong to abort a healthy post-24-week-old human foetus, without accepting that it was equally wrong to fail to conceive such a foetus. Tooley's argument at this point is only plausible though if one accepts that there are no morally significant differences between potential and possible persons. If this were so, then it would indeed seem to follow that failing to actualise possible persons and destroying potential persons were morally equivalent acts. But, I will argue, if post-24-week-old human foetuses have an interest in continued existence on the basis of their being the same enduring subject of experience as the persons they will become, then potential persons and possible persons are not morally equivalent beings. In which case, Tooley's application of the Principle of Moral Symmetry to a pair of cases, one of which is a potential person, the other of which is a possible person is misleading. There is no symmetry between the two cases, and hence one can clearly differentiate between the moral significance of destroying one and failing to actualise the other. This being so, I will go on to say, there is no inconsistency to be found in supporting the argument from potential presented here, whilst denying that it is wrong to fail to actualise possible persons.

Following this I will look at the overall consequences of the argument developed in the first seven chapters. Firstly, I will argue that as the human embryo neither manifests the psychological capacities of an actual person, nor has an active potential to become a person, it cannot be the holder of an interest in continued existence. The human embryo is neither a being with the capacity to experience its world, nor a being that is psychologically continuous with the person it one day becomes. Consequently, to abort a human embryo is not to destroy a being with a right to life. Similarly, I will argue that arguments against IVF and embryo experimentation that are based on an argument from potential also fail.

Secondly, I will look directly at the issue of abortion. Abortion, as it is now practised, I will claim, is in many cases a direct infringement of the foetal interests considered in previous chapters. Current abortion practices, therefore, should in many cases be replaced with procedures that take both the mother's and the foetus's interests into consideration. And, if this were the case, even if sufficient justification could be provided in specific cases to warrant the over-riding of a post-24-week-old foetus's interest in continuing to exist, its capacity to suffer would make the causing of its death in a painful way morally wrong in the vast majority of cases. Moreover, similar consequences may also follow from an acknowledgment of a pre-24-week-old foetus's interests.

Finally, I will address the conflict that can potentially arise between a foetus's and its mother's interests, and the consequent issues that have to be considered in the determination of whether an abortion is the right thing to do in a given set of circumstances. The inevitability that such conflicts will occasionally arise does not, I will argue, detract from the argument presented in the body of this discussion. While there may well be times in which a woman's interests will justifiably override a foetus's interests, the possibility that the foetus could suffer greatly in our efforts to preserve the mother's life should not be allowed to become an obsolete consideration: at such times our desire to minimise suffering ought to give us reason to pause and reflect on the interests of all concerned – including those of the unborn.

2 Potential and Physical Dependence

Types of Potential

A common response to an argument from potential is to ask why a human foetus's potential to become a person is morally significant, while the potential of an unfertilised ovum to become a person is not morally significant. The answer lies in the fundamental distinction between the types of potential each of these entities possesses. In the case of the human foetus the potential possessed is a potential to become, whilst in the case of the ovum there is only a potential to produce. And, as Buckle pointed out, the reason why this is a morally relevant distinction is because "the process of actualising the potential to become preserves some form of individual identity...[while the] potential to produce...does not require any form of identity to be preserved".[1] Another way to put this same distinction is in Tooley's terms of active, latent, and passive potential.

Tooley's explanation of active potential corresponds closely with Buckle's view of the "potential to become", which Buckle defines as "the power possessed by an entity to undergo changes which are changes to *itself* ...to undergo growth or better still development".[2] Active potential is in many ways similar to this. In Tooley's words:

> An entity may be said to have an active potential for acquiring some property P if there are within it all of the positive causal factors needed to bring it about that it will acquire property P, and there are no other factors present within it that will block the action of the positive ones.[3]

Tooley's focus on "positive causal factors" in this definition is significant and requires further investigation. However, given the complexity of the

---
[1] Stephen Buckle, (1990) 'Arguing From Potential', pp. 90-108 of Peter Singer *et al. Embryo Experimentation*, Cambridge University Press, Cambridge, p. 95.
[2] Buckle, *ibid.*
[3] Tooley, *op. cit.* p. 167.

causality debate, and the space that would be required to do justice to that debate, only a general understanding of the term can be provided here. For the sake of this discussion the positive causal factors of personhood will be understood to be those positive factors that must necessarily be present for the manifestation of personhood, and that if absent will prevent the manifestation of personhood.[4] Some examples may serve to make the meaning of this concept clearer. They will also serve to highlight why it is that I believe Tooley's conception of "positive causal factors" to be too broad a category to be relevant to the potentiality debate.

If one considers an apple tree seedling and the positive causal factors required for it to become an adult fruit-bearing tree, one would, given Tooley's use of "positive causal factors", list not only the genetic make-up and internal physiology of the seedling, but also the external factors required to ensure an adequate supply of nutrients and therefore growth – water, sunshine, oxygen, and so on – as positive causal factors that are necessary for the seedling to develop into an adult tree.

While such an exposition would be detailed, it has the potential to continue almost indefinitely. As Mackie said:

> ...it is impossible, without including in the cause the whole environment, the whole state of the universe (and so excluding any likelihood of repetition), to find a generally sufficient condition, one which is "by itself" adequate to secure the effect.[5]

A line must therefore be drawn between those factors which are central to the issue at hand, and those that are extraneous. A listing of the positive causal factors related to the development of a seedling into an adult tree, for example, that was as inclusive as that pointed to by Mackie would severely limit the cases it is applicable too. Furthermore, it would contribute little of substance to our understanding of the intrinsic properties required for a seedling to develop into a tree. For this reason, a

---

[4] The explanations given here will focus only on Tooley's use of the term, and are by necessity far briefer than that which Tooley would provide. Tooley's complex theory of causation, which provides a much more detailed exposition of his ideas than I can do justice to can be found in Michael Tooley (1987) *Causation: a realist approach*, Oxford University Press, Oxford.

[5] J.L. Mackie (1975) 'Cause and Conditions', pp. 15-38 of Ernest Sosa (ed.) *Causes and Conditionals*, Oxford University Press, London, p. 23.

causal field (that is, a set of background features that are given as existing) must be agreed upon.

In general conversation the causal field is defined by the context of the discussion and it is rarely explicitly mentioned. In cases such as the one at hand however, in which the constituents of the casual field can have a significant effect on the conclusions reached, it is necessary to explicitly define and justify the contents of the background causal field.

It is at this point, in the determination of which factors ought to be part of the causal field, that I disagree with Tooley. The distinction is an important one, for it is in the exclusion of factors from the background causal field that one implicitly defines those factors as central to the specific causation issue at hand. As Mackie pointed out though, it is generally "...an arbitrary matter whether a particular feature is regarded as a condition [that is, a positive causal factor] or as part of the field...".[6] One could therefore, as Tooley would do, exclude the external requirements of the seedling from the causal field concerned with its development into a tree, and thus define them as positive causal factors. Or, alternatively, one could include such external requirements in the causal field, and focus only on the internal factors required for a seedling to develop into a tree. I propose to do the latter.

The reason for this is that if I were to take as positive causal factors all the internal and the external factors relating to the seedling's development, it would be implausible to suggest that any biological organism could possess an active potential (for personhood or anything else) in anything other than a momentary way. All biological organisms are dependent on the external world for the meeting of their physiological needs, and all are susceptible to damage if these needs are not met: a seedling could not become a tree if it was not supplied with water; a kitten could not become a cat if it was not nurtured and fed during its first few weeks of existence; and a human child could not become an adult if it were not protected and nurtured during its first few years of life. In each of these cases there could be no active potential if the external factors described were treated as positive causal factors. The same is true of all other biological organisms: no biological organism could possess an active potential, were all of the external conditions required for its development defined as positive causal factors. In which case, the notion of "active potential" would become

---

[6] *Ibid.*

morally irrelevant. It is for this reason that Tooley's understanding of positive causal factors needs to be restricted if it is to have any place within the context of biological development and moral significance.

Consequently, while Tooley would argue that a seedling does not possess all of the positive casual factors required for it to develop into an adult tree, because it must necessarily obtain water and nutrients from its external world – and while I agree with him given his definition of the causal field – I would argue that given a causal field that encompasses all of the external necessities, a healthy seedling would possess *all of the positive causal factors needed to bring it about that it will* develop into an adult tree so long as it was genetically and physically sound, and could consequently effectively utilise the necessary external requirements were it afforded the opportunity to do so. If such were the case, no additional factors central to our understanding of seedlings and trees would have to be added to the seedling's intrinsic properties for it to develop into an adult tree, and the seedling would, as a result be both numerically and ontologically identical to the mature tree it becomes.[7]

Closely related to active potential is latent potential. An entity has a latent potential, says Tooley, if "...all of the positive factors are present within it, but there is some feature of it that will block the action of those factors".[8] The previously mentioned apple tree sapling would be an example of an entity with a latent potential if, for example, it had inherited a genetic disorder that prevented it from developing into a mature tree (it could, perhaps, have acquired a disorder that prevents it from flowering normally, and consequently from bearing fruit). In such a case, even though the sapling may possess *all of the positive factors required for it to develop into a mature tree, there is a negative factor within it that will block the action of the positive factors*. Consequently, there will never be a mature fruit tree that is both numerically and ontologically identical to the sapling.

Finally, an entity has a passive potential for acquiring property P, says Tooley, "...if other things could act upon it in such a way as to bring it about that it acquires property P".[9] Passive potential, as can be seen,

---

[7] The retention of identity beyond mere numerical identity is central to our understanding of a being's moral standing, and will be returned to in some detail in Chapter Four.
[8] Tooley, *op. cit.*
[9] *Ibid.*

closely parallels Buckle's view of the "potential to produce".[10] To see an example of passive potential we must go further back in the process of development than the previously mentioned sapling. An entity with a passive potential to become a fruit tree is an entity that is missing one or more properties that are necessary for it to develop into a fruit tree. Hence, it is the unfertilised male and female nuclei (the pollen grain and ovary respectively) of the parent trees that possess a passive potential to become a fruit tree. Together they can produce a seedling, and eventually that seedling may become a mature fruit tree. But, so long as the germ cells remain separate, neither possesses *all of the positive causal factors needed to bring about* the development of a fruit tree. In which case neither the pollen grain nor the ovary can be numerically or ontologically identical to the fruit tree that results from their union.

As can be seen from the above examples, whichever account of potential is accepted (Tooley's or Buckle's) it remains the case that it is only an active potential to become a person can grant a being the moral relevance of a person.[11] Why? Because it is only in the case of an active potential that the potential person necessarily possesses within it all of the morally relevant factors necessary to become an actual person, and no factors to prevent it becoming a person. Thus, only a being with an active potential to become a person would necessarily retain a form of identity greater than mere numerical identity throughout its development into an actual person.[12]

In the case of a latent potential, whilst it is true that a latent person would have all of the positive causal factors necessary for it to become an actual person, those factors would be prevented from becoming manifest, and the being could not therefore become a person prior to the removal of

---

[10] Buckle, *op. cit.*

[11] It is important to reiterate here that on Tooley's account of active potential, which adopts a broad understanding of positive causal factors, and hence a narrow view of the background causal field, this would not be the case. From Tooley's perspective no form of potential can grant a being the moral significance of an actual person, because no form of potential would ensure the presence of the required identity relations between the potential and actual person. The account of active potential that is argued for in this paper is narrower than presented by Tooley however, in that all of the external requirements of personhood are taken to be a part of the background causal field.

[12] The account of personal identity being utilised here is found in Derek Parfit (1984) *Reasons and Persons*, Clarendon Press, Oxford. Parfit's argument will be discussed in some detail in Chapter Four.

the negative factors. And, were those factors to be removed, the being's potential to become a person would be transformed from a latent potential to an active potential. In the case of a passive potential, something would first need to be added to the being's intrinsic properties before it could become an actual person. In which case the properties of the actual person would not be identical to those of the being with the passive potential. It is only if the properties required for the being to become a person were added to its original properties that the entity that results would be able to develop into a person. In which case, the resulting entity would no longer possess a passive potential; it would possess an active potential to become a person.

Foetal Potential

Tooley's first challenge to an argument from potential grounding a foetus's right to continued existence, focuses on the possibility of a human foetus possessing an active potential to become a person. As was seen above, Tooley's view of active potential includes the external as well as the internal causal factors required for personhood. And, because his claim is one that, if correct, would prove the argument from potential to be irrelevant to the abortion debate it is necessary to spend some time here detailing why Tooley believes a foetus's physical dependence on the external world ought to be placed within the category of positive causal factors required for personhood. It is Tooley's claim that human foetuses cannot have an active potential to become persons, because they are dependent on others for the provision of sustenance and for the meeting of their environmental requirements. A human foetus's potential, in other words, is, according to Tooley, only a passive potential: a potential that requires additional external factors before it can become manifest. If this claim were correct, then even if I were to show that the argument from potential were a valid argument, and that it does not fall foul of the errors Tooley believes it does, I could not show that the human foetus was (other things being equal) a morally relevant potential person. I do not believe that Tooley is correct though. Once the external requirements of the human foetus are removed from the field of positive causal factors and placed instead within the causal field that is given to be present in all cases, it becomes clear that a human foetus can possess an active potential to become a person, even though it is dependent on others for the satisfaction of its physiological needs.

Tooley interprets the term "potential person" as an entity that will, if not interfered with, develop into a person.[13] But, he argues, given that some foetuses clearly would not develop into persons without the assistance of other people (specifically he is talking here of those born prematurely), it cannot merely be a matter of not interfering with their development, one must actively support them if they are to survive and develop into persons.[14] Furthermore, as it cannot be the case that a foetus's intrinsic properties change with its environment, if some foetuses do not have all of the properties required for them to develop into persons, then it must be the case that no foetuses have within them all the necessary properties to become persons. As Tooley says, human foetuses will develop into persons only if treated in certain ways and provided with certain substances, consequently they cannot possess an active potential to become persons, for they cannot have within them all of the positive causal factors necessary to become persons.

Thus, he claims, human foetuses cannot be the holders of a fully active potential to become persons. Indeed, by Tooley's definition human foetuses and infants must have only a passive potential to become persons. For, within the background causal field defined by Tooley human foetuses and infants would only become persons if other persons acted upon them in such a way as to bring it about that they became persons. Moreover, such would, within Tooley's background causal field, be the case for the first two or three years of a child's life. For, it is not only the human foetus that is dependent on others for the meeting of its physiological needs, so too are human infants and toddlers.[15]

Tooley goes on to suggest that although passive potentials can range from "almost active" (in which "nearly all of the positive factors are present in the entity"), to almost totally passive ("in which nearly all the relevant factors have to be added...."), it is implausible to suggest that any form of passive potential is morally relevant. This is so because if one were to attempt to define some passive potentials as morally relevant, and other passive potentials as morally irrelevant, one would find it incredibly

---

[13] Tooley, *op.cit.* p. 166.
[14] *Ibid.*
[15] This is not a claim that Tooley actually states, it does however appear to follow given his line of reasoning.

difficult to specify a clear and non-arbitrary boundary between that which ought to be morally considerable and that that need not be morally considered.[16] Consequently, according to Tooley's argument even if one were to accept that an active potential is morally considerable,[17] a human foetus could in no way be morally relevant due to its potential to become a person; and neither could a human infant or toddler given this line of reasoning. Not only are they not the possessors of an active potential to become a person, but the type of potential they do possess is indistinguishable from other morally irrelevant forms of potential.

It appears to me, though, that the type of potential a human foetus has to become a person could be an active potential.[18] Tooley's background causal field, as has been mentioned, does not include the foetus's physical requirements; if the causal field is redefined however it could be the case that a human foetus does possess all of the morally significant positive causal factors required for it to have an active potential to become a person. Why though, should the background causal field be redefined? Would not the resulting causal field be just as arbitrary as Tooley's choice of causal field? I will show that far from being arbitrary, a redefinition of the causal field is a logical consequence of the issue being considered.

The physical properties of a person are not the defining features of personhood, thus logically they cannot, without argument, be assumed to be defining features of potential personhood. If, as Tooley suggests, personhood is definable only in terms of a being's past or presently exercised psychological states, then there is no requirement for a being to possess any specific relation to its physical surroundings in order for it to be a person.[19] Consequently, there is no reason to suggest that a being's potential to become a person is dependent on its holding a specific relation to the physical world either. I would suggest that a potential person's relationship to the physical world is as irrelevant to the determination of its

---

[16] *Ibid.*

[17] Though, of course, to reiterate Tooley's argument, even an active potential would not in itself make a being morally considerable.

[18] At this stage I am concerned only with the logical possibility of a human foetus possessing an active potential to become a person. The more specific question concerning what causal factors would necessarily have to be present for a being to have an active potential to become a person, and when a human foetus might manifest these properties will be addressed in the following chapter.

[19] Tooley's conception of personhood and the specific psychological capacities it encompasses will be discussed in detail in Chapter Five.

moral standing, as is an actual person's relationship to the physical world. In determining a potential person's moral standing it is only those factors that are necessary for its continued development into a person, given its continued physical existence, that are morally relevant. In other words, I suggest that a distinction be made between the addition of factors that will alter or add to a being's morally relevant psychological properties, and the addition of factors that simply allow a being to maintain its existence.

In the case of a human foetus it is only the latter that its dependence on others entails. In supplying a foetus with food and an appropriate living environment, one is not adding anything to, or taking away from, its psychological capacities: one is simply attempting to ensure its continued existence. It is at this point that I believe we ought to set the limits of the causal field - those physical factors that simply ensure a foetus's or person's continued existence ought to be considered as a part of the background causal field, while those psychological factors that are essential to the development and continuation of a person ought to be considered as positive causal factors of personhood. And, given this enlarged causal field there is no reason to suppose that a foetus's dependence on others for the meeting of its physical needs means that it cannot possess all the positive causal factors necessary for it to develop into a person.

Some concrete examples will serve to highlight why the distinction ought to be made in this way. Consider, for instance, the case of an actual person who in some way comes to be totally dependent on others for his/her physical sustenance. Let's suppose that a woman was involved in a serious accident that left her in an intensive care ward, and totally dependent on others for the meeting of her physical needs. So long as she retained the ability to see herself as a continuing being over time, her existence as a person would be unaffected by her new physical status. As persons, we are all dependent on others to a greater or lesser degree for our personal well being, and clearly the degree of dependence is mutable – it can change rapidly depending on circumstance. But, neither our identity nor our intrinsic properties change as a result of an alteration in mere physical circumstance. It is only when our psychological capacities are added to, or taken away from, that our moral status may change. In the above case, even though the woman comes to be dependent upon others for her survival, the things supplied to her by others are not things that will affect who or what she is. Though she will not survive if others do not supply her with food and care, the supply of these things does not alter her essential properties: her personhood is merely maintained, it is not altered. The continuation of her life would at this point depend totally on others, just as does a foetus's, but her moral status as a person would remain unchanged. She would not be any less a person because her body was in a state of greater dependency.

This being so, why cannot the same be true of a potential person? Clearly, the degree of physical dependence does not affect an actual person's intrinsic properties, so how is it that it can affect a potential person's intrinsic properties? I do not believe it does. Consider, for example, two healthy, genetically normal seedlings, one of which is growing in the wild, in a position in which it can satisfy all of the physical requirements that are necessary for it to develop into a tree without external assistance, the other of which is growing indoors as a household plant. The latter is certainly dependent on another being for its survival and continued growth and development into a tree. But, surely, these two seedlings do not differ in their intrinsic properties. If the one in the wild possesses an active potential to become a tree, so too must the one indoors. Does the one in the wild possess an active potential to become a tree? Yes, if one takes the causal field to be those external physical conditions necessary for its survival, and the positive causal factors to be those internal properties that are intrinsic to the seedling, I believe that it does. All the relevant positive causal factors that are necessary for it to develop into a tree would be present within it, and no other factors would be present within it to block the action of the positive ones. Of course, it may not achieve its potential, there may be a drought, a bush fire, the area in which it is growing may be logged – any number of things could happen to prevent the manifestation of its potential. Nevertheless, so long as it possesses within itself all the relevant internal properties that are necessary for it to become a tree, it has an active potential to become a tree.

Is the seedling indoors any different? No. Its intrinsic properties are identical to those of the wild seedling, only its environment is different. As a household plant it is totally dependent on others for the meeting of its physiological requirements, and consequently any number of things could happen to prevent the manifestation of its potential. But, if its intrinsic properties are identical to those of the wild seedling, then it too must possess within it all of the positive causal factors necessary for it to become a tree. Its dependence on another for its physical well being could not change its intrinsic properties, it would merely mean that if another did not meet its physical requirements it would not survive. This however does not alter its nature.

The human foetus is similar to this in some ways, while there are times when a foetus is in its natural environment and needs no further assistance in order to continue its development, there are other times when such is not the case, and it comes to be totally dependent on others for the continuation of its life. Tooley sees the possibility of such dependence as a sign that all foetuses are lacking in the necessary causal factors required to become persons. But, as we can see in the case of the two seedlings this is too strong a test to apply to biological organisms. One needs, within a debate concerning moral standing, to be able to distinguish between those factors that are morally relevant and those that are not. One way to do this is in the way discussed here. We do not in the normal course of conversation interpret the possibility of a seedling's dependence on another as a sign that no seedling could possess all of the positive causal factors required to become a tree. Neither should we do so in the case of a human foetus. When the things supplied by another person are merely those that allow the potential entity to continue its development, when these things do not affect the entity's intrinsic properties, the entity in question can still possess an active potential. If a seedling can possess an active potential to become a tree, despite the possibility of it not achieving that potential because it is totally dependent on another for the meeting of its needs, so too a human foetus's potential could be an active potential to become a person despite the possibility of it being totally dependent on others for its survival.

Does a foetus actually have an active potential to become a person though? This is a separate issue, the answer to which is dependent on whether, given its continued physical development, all of the positive causal factors necessary for personhood are present within it. This is the question I will turn to next. What are the necessary properties required for an active potential to become a person? Does a human foetus acquire these properties as it develops, or does it have them from the moment it begins its existence? While these questions are yet to be addressed, what we do know is that despite its dependence on others for its survival (for the meeting of its environmental and nutritional needs) a human foetus can logically possess an active potential to become a person.

Personhood, as Tooley says, is definable in terms of the being's past or presently exercised psychological states, and as such the factors that are defined as positive causal factors necessary for personhood ought to be those directly associated with the manifestation of those psychological capacities; they should not include the morally irrelevant physical characteristics of the being that are shared with all biological organisms. This being so, the possibility that a human foetus may require another to meet its physiological needs would not detract from the possibility that the positive causal factors required for personhood may be a part of the human foetus.

3 Foetal Physiology and Active Potential

The Necessary Properties

What then are the morally relevant causal factors that lead to personhood, and does a human foetus come to possess them prior to its birth? These two questions form the focus of this chapter. As will become clear, there are no definitive answers to these questions. There is, however, some fairly widespread agreement as to the possibilities. The first, and most apparent positive causal factor that is necessary for personhood is an appropriate genetic structure.[1] Whilst it is generally accepted that self-awareness (the capacity to see oneself as a distinct and continuing being over time) and hence personhood, is largely a result of an individual's social interaction, the right genetic makeup is, without a doubt, also necessary. Without a species-typical genetic structure mere existence in a social world would not result in humans becoming persons. This becomes clear if we consider the numerous other species, such as our domestic dogs and cats, which evidently do interact on a social level, yet do not become self-aware as a result of that interaction.

Even though an appropriate genetic structure is a necessary positive causal factor for personhood in the case of a human foetus however, its presence is not sufficient to ensure the development of personhood. "The presence of a single biological entity", as Burgess and Tawia pointed out,

> ...is the physical precondition for the presence of a person; a functioning nervous system is a presupposition for physical activity; an integrated nervous system is required for intellectual activity. But these biological realities neither guarantee the presence of nor constitute the definition of a person.[2]

---

[1] I hesitate to label such genetic make-up as "normal", as there are many deviations from the norm to be found in the human genome, that do not affect the manifestation of personhood.

[2] J.A. Burgess and S.A. Tawia (1996) 'When did you first begin to feel it? – Locating the beginning of human consciousness', pp. 1-26 of *Bioethics*, v.10(1), Jan.

And, if as Burgess and Tawia say, biological factors alone will not guarantee the presence of personhood, further non-genetic factors must also be required. This brings us to a second positive causal factor necessary for the development of personhood: the ability to interact with the social world, and the ability to learn from that interaction.[3] As I mentioned above, it is commonly accepted that self-awareness, a differentiation between oneself and others, is a result of interaction with others. In Eisenberg's words, "there is no mental function without brain and social context. To ask how much of mind is biological and how much is social is as meaningless as to ask how much of the area of a rectangle is due to its width and how much to its height...".[4] A person, in other words, is not a result of a one-dimensional process. Just as a rectangle would not exist without two dimensions – width and height, a person would not exist without both biology and social context.

It could perhaps be argued that to talk of the necessity of the social world for personhood is to alter the understanding of personhood that is being utilised, from Tooley's psychological view to a more sociological view. This is not the case however.

To say that a person would not exist without a social context is not to define persons solely in terms of their social relations, rather it is to say that the necessary psychological state required for the existence of personhood: namely, the ability to see oneself as a continuing being over time, is the result of a genetic predisposition for self-awareness coupled with prolonged social interaction. One explanation of the role of social interaction in the development of personhood is provided by Hegel in his discussion of selfhood. As he says:

---

[3] It has been suggested that in order for there to be social interaction there must be other people, and that it is difficult to discriminate between other people and nutrition and warmth as all are external factors required for a being's development into a person. It should be noted, however, that there is a logical distinction to be made between the people with whom a being interacts and the internal capacity to interact with those people. It is the internal capacity to interact that is being categorised as a positive causal factor for personhood. The actual social world and the persons that exist within are taken to be a part of the background causal field: that is, they are assumed to be present within the context of the discussion at hand.

[4] Leon Eisenberg (1995) 'The Social Construction of the Human Brain', pp. 1563-1569 of *American Journal of Psychiatry*, v.152(11), Nov. p. 1565.

The self only becomes the self through action. That which is externalised is then internalised, and the self that becomes the self through interaction with other selves and in the projection onto the world of its inwardness, reintegrates that which flowed out to reach its next stage of development.[5]

To put this another way, there is a dynamic interdependency between the human subject and the social world, such that self-awareness, and hence personhood, is a result of a human being's continual experiencing of the world, and the integration into itself of the results which that experience has on both itself and the world. The person that results from this process cannot be disassociated from either the social or the biological – both are essential parts of its being. Thus whilst a genetic predisposition may provide a human foetus with the biological basis for personhood, that basic predisposition would never become a reality if there were no social interaction following birth. Physiological, psychological, and social developments are in this way all closely interdependent: each requiring the others in order to manifest their full potential.[6]

Even if we limit the examination of the development of personhood to its manifest biological features we discover that the manifold alterations in neural pathways, the ever increasing number of synaptic connections, and the removal of unused connections, that precede personhood, are dependent on an infant's interaction with his/her social environment. As Wiesel put it, "genes controlling embryonic development shape the structure of the infant brain; the infant's experience in the world, then fine-tunes the pattern of neural connections underlying the brain's function".[7] If the human infant did not first experience the world on a psychological level, it would not undergo these changes in brain structure, and without the increasing complexity that comes with these changes, the infant would

---

[5] See G.W.F. Hegel (1954) 'The Phenomenology of Spirit', in Friedrich, Carl J. (ed.) *The Philosophy of Hegel*, Modern Library, New York.

[6] To talk of the need for social interaction is not to say that only humans could provide the necessary social interaction required for the development of personhood. It is plausible to suppose that a differentiation between oneself and others' and perhaps a concept of oneself continuing over time could result from prolonged interaction with a variety of species other than human beings. The point being made is only that without lengthy interaction with some form of social beings, human infants could not become persons.

[7] Wiesel cited in Eisenberg, *op.cit.*

not become a self-aware being.[8] Thus, whilst an appropriate genetic structure is a necessary positive causal factor in the human foetus's development into a person it is not sufficient; social interaction is also necessary.

In order to interact with the social world though, a foetus must first be conscious – not merely sentient in that it can experience the physical sensations of its environment, although that too is necessary – but a deeper level of consciousness, a psychological awareness of its world and an ability to respond to that world. For it is only after the human foetus is psychologically aware of its environment that it can possess the properties necessary to interact with the social world. Without the manifestation of each and every one of these capacities the human foetus could not become a person.

Without the right genetic structure a human foetus could not become sentient; prior to the actual manifestation of sentience it could not become aware of its environment on a conscious level; prior to a conscious awareness of its environment the human foetus could not begin to interact with, and learn from, its social world; and without interaction and participation in a social world a human infant could not become a person. Consequently, the manifestation of all of these capacities – an appropriate genetic structure, physical sentience, consciousness, and an ability to interact with the social world – are the minimum positive causal factors required for a foetus to have an active potential to become a person. There is no one factor that is both necessary and sufficient for potential personhood. Rather, there is a complex and multidimensional set of factors, and it is only if a human foetus manifests all of them that it can possess an active potential to become a person.

To manifest some, but not all, of these capacities is not sufficient. For instance, the human embryo may manifest an appropriate genetic structure, but on the basis of that factor alone it cannot develop into a person. Its potential to become a person at that stage would be at most a latent potential. Its genetic structure may contain the information necessary for it

---

[8] Whilst the primacy I am according to the social world has been challenged by some, it appears to me that no matter what other complex properties are pointed to, be it rationality, language, or abstract thought, none are possible in a social vacuum. Each of these capacities, and many others, are inherently social in nature, and without the manifest capacity to interact with its social environment (be that human or otherwise), a human infant could not develop these capacities.

to become sensate and conscious of its surroundings, but the lack of expression of this genetic information acts to prevent the foetus from becoming self-aware. And, as we have seen a latent potential is not sufficient for a being to be morally relevant on the basis of its relationship with the person develops into. Consequently, if a human foetus's interest in continued existence rests upon its potential personhood, a human foetus must manifest all of the above factors before it can possess such an interest; only then would it have an active potential to become a person, and only then would it possess the relevant moral status as a direct result of that potential. It should be stressed at this point that the manifestation of all of these capacities would be insufficient for actual personhood. The most sophisticated psychological capacity that is demanded by this explication of active potential for personhood is an ability to interact with the social world. This capacity is far below the self-awareness that is required for actual personhood. To be able to interact with others does not demand a capacity to see oneself as a continuing being over time. Hence, a human foetus could not be an actual person on the basis of its manifestation of the capacities discussed in this chapter.

Physical Foetal Development

The question to be asked then is when, if at all, does a foetus manifest these capacities? Clearly, a human foetus either begins its existence with an appropriate genetic structure or it never acquires one, but when does a foetus become sentient, when is it consciously aware of its environment, and when does it begin to interact with its social world? To answer this, it is necessary to look at the developmental stages of a human foetus. Below is a table that sets out each of the relevant physiological changes that occur during the human foetus's development. As becomes clear when looking at the information contained in the table, biology alone will not tell us exactly when a foetus becomes conscious, or if a foetus has a capacity to interact with the social world prior to its birth. Indeed, the conflicting literature on the topic highlights the problematic nature of the question. For, whilst researchers and theorists consistently agree upon the biological facts, a clear and objective statement concerning the development of consciousness is much harder to discover.

By 20 weeks post-conception the "network which conveys pain in humans (the spino-thalamic system) is fully established and connected", and the final connections between this system and the cortex are completed during the next four weeks.[9] The question that arises in response to this biological reality, however, is whether the spino-thalamic system is sufficient for a human foetus to be conscious or to feel pain, or whether a functioning cortex is also necessary. According to Fitzgerald, a functioning cortex is necessary; "pain is an emotion", she says, "and without higher level connections no emotion is possible". Therefore, she concludes, "it is not possible for a foetus to feel pain prior to the connections to the cortex being established".[10]

But, Fitzgerald goes on to say, it is possible that the nervous system of the foetus is wired up to maximise the inputs that come in,[11] and it is just this possibility that her dissenters argue for. According to Fitzgerald's opponents in the debate over foetal pain, it may well be the case that the foetal nervous system functions differently to the adult nervous system; it may be that the specific functions of the higher brain structures in the adult nervous system are temporarily undertaken by the more primitive brain structures which develop first. As Noonan says, "the general sense organs begin to differentiate between 90 and 120 days. But, as responses to touch, pressure and light precede this period visible differentiation must be preceded by a period in which the general sense organs are functioning".[12]

---

[9] Paul Ranalli, 'Abortion and the Unborn Baby: The Painful Truth', at *http://www.california.prolife/paintrut.htm*. Although this is clearly an anti-abortion site, and therefore contains literature in support of that cause, Ranalli is well qualified in this area, being both a neurologist at the University of Toronto, and an executive member of the De Veber Institute for Bioethics and Social Research.

[10] Fitzgerald, quoted in 'The Problem of Pain: A Report by the Commission of Inquiry into Foetal Sentience', *op. cit.* (page number unavailable). See also, Adrian R. Lloyd-Thomas & Maria Fitzgerald (1996) 'For Debate: Reflex Responses do not Necessarily Signify Pain', pp. 797-798 of *The British Medical Journal*, V.313, 28 September. The issue of pain in foetuses has been focused on as an indicator of consciousness throughout this discussion for two reasons. Firstly, it appears to be the most thoroughly researched area of foetal neurological and psychological development, and secondly because it is possible that the concept of pain - it possessing both a physical and emotional component - can help to determine how the term consciousness is being interpreted in the various arguments that have been put forward.

[11] Fitzgerald, *ibid.* (page number unavailable).

[12] John T Noonan (1981) 'The Experience of Pain by the Unborn', pp. 205-216 of Thomas Hilgers *et al.* (eds.) *New Perspectives on Abortion*, Aletheia Books, Maryland, p. 210.

Table 1: The Physiological Development of the Human Foetus[13]

Age Post-Menstrual in weeks	Age Post-Conceptional in weeks	Comment	Reference
4.5	2.5	Development of spinal cord and brain begins	Kuljis (1994)
6	4	Nerves start to grow, no connections reported between them	Okado (1981)
7	5	First observed synapses between neurones	Okado (1981)
7	5	First fibers arrive in the cerebral vesicles. Start to form the primordial plexiform layer	Marin-Padilla et al. (1982)
7.5	5.5	Earliest reported foetal movements	De Vries et al. (1982)
8.5	6.5	Head, trunk, and pelvis move away from a stimulus	De Vries et al. (1982)
9	7	Electrical activity detected in developing brain stem	Brokowski & Berstine (1955)
10	8	Development of higher brain begins	Marin-Padilla (1978)
10	8	Synapse formation within spine	Okado (1981)
10-11	8-9	Isolated foetal breathing movements	De Vries et al. (1982)
10-11	8-9	Initial development of thalamus	McCullagh (1996)
			(continued...)

---

[13] This table is taken from 'The Problem of Pain: A Report by the Commission of Inquiry into Foetal Sentience' (1996) at *http://www.care .org.uk/issues/fs/hs05.htm*, which was commissioned by the House of Lords, London. (There are a considerable number of references to this report throughout this text, unfortunately, due to the nature of internet publications, page numbers cannot be provided.) The reason for stopping this table at 28 weeks rather than continuing through till 38 weeks is that the period following 28 weeks is one of consolidation and physical growth: neither the physiological state of the nervous system, nor the foetus's behaviour undergo further dramatic changes after 28 weeks of development.

26 *Interests in Abortion*

Table 1 Continued

11	9	Stimulation of hands causes partial finger closure	De Vries *et al.* (1982)
12.5	10.5	Stimulation of lips elicits reflex swallowing	De Vries *et al.* (1982)
13	11	Sensory receptors on hands, feet and face	Humphrey (1964)
16	14	Episodes of regular foetal breathing movements	De Vries *et al.* (1982)
20-22	18-20	Nerves connect between cortex and thalamus	Laroche (1981)
20	18	Electrical activity recorded in the thalamus	Bergstrom (1969)
22	20	Sensory receptors on all skin surfaces	Humphrey (1964)
23	21	Mount hormonal stress response to needle placement for blood transfusions	Giannakoulopoulos *et al.* (1994)
26	24	Sensory input can reach cortex – therefore pain signals could reach areas of consciousness	Fitzgerald (1995)
30	28	Myelination complete in main pathways	Gilles *et al.* (1983)

In a similar way, it has been argued, it is possible that consciousness exists prior to the development of the organs known to be responsible for consciousness in adults. For instance, it is possible, Glover argues, that there is consciousness of pain between 12-25 weeks just with thalamic activity. Such experience would be generalised rather than clearly defined: not through clear, sharp pain pathways as found in adult humans, but via different mechanisms.[14] Indeed, it is possible some say, that a pre-24-week-old foetus feels even greater pain than does a later-term foetus, as the

---

[14] Vivette Glover, cited in 'The Problem of Pain: A Report by the Commission of Inquiry into Foetal Sentience', *op.cit.* (page number unavailable).

spino-thalamic system is functioning, yet the cortical connections which serve to mediate the responses felt in adults, are not yet present.[15]

It is difficult to determine the truth of the matter based on these conflicting interpretations. But, perhaps this is because the meanings given to "consciousness" are different in the two cases. On the one side is Fitzgerald and her counter-parts (see Burgess and Tawia, and the Royal College of Obstetricians and Gynaecologists)[16] who argue that in order for a foetus to be conscious, the cortex, as the centre of awareness in adult humans, must be functioning. From their perspective, consciousness appears to denote a psychological or emotional awareness. For instance, Lloyd-Thomas and Fitzgerald in their discussion of the issue state that, "...the brain must achieve a certain level of neural functioning, as well as having prior experience, before pain can be understood".[17] In which case, as they say, a functioning cortex would appear to be a requisite property of foetal consciousness. And, as most theorists agree a human foetus possesses a functioning cortex by 26 weeks post-conception this would point to the development of foetal consciousness at around 26 weeks post-conception. This time-frame is explicitly stated by Fitzgerald who says that, "to feel pain one needs input to the cortex which begins at 23 weeks and is sufficient by 26 weeks to allow continuous communication between the higher and lower brain".[18]

Positioned on the opposite side of the debate to Fitzgerald sit Glover and like-minded theorists such as Fisk, Noonan, and Liley,[19] who argue that a functioning thalamus may be all that is required for consciousness. This interpretation of consciousness does not seem to imply any emotional awareness or understanding; it is focused, as Noonan makes clear, purely on physical sensations. In Noonan's words:

---

[15] Peter Hepper cited in Glover *ibid.* (page number unavailable).
[16] See Burgess and Tawia, *op cit.* and the Royal College of Obstetricians and Gynaecologists (1997) *Foetal Awareness: report of a working party*, RCOG Press, London.
[17] *op. cit.* p. 797.
[18] Fitzgerald, *op.cit.* (page number unavailable). The confusion that could arise with a two week difference in foetal age being found throughout the literature on foetal development is a result of some theorists speaking in terms of post-conception age, and others speaking in terms of post-menstrual age.
[19] See Fisk, cited in 'The Problem of Pain: A Report by the Commission of Inquiry into Foetal Sentience', *op.cit.* (page number unavailable); Noonan, *op cit.*; And Sir William Liley, 'A Day in the Life of the Foetus', pp. 29-35 of Thomas Hilgers *et al., op. cit.*

>...we say that sense receptors are there because there is a response to touch, and taste receptors because there is a response to taste. By the same token we are able to say that pain receptors are present when evasive action follows the intrusion of pressure or light, or when injection of a disagreeable fluid lowers the rate of swallowing.[20]

Such a focus seems to be concerned only with raw physical experience, not the vastly more complex emotional understanding of pain that Lloyd-Thomas and Fitzgerald appear to be speaking of. This suggests that there are two distinct understandings of consciousness at play in the debate.

Is there any physiological or psychological basis for such a difference in the interpretation of consciousness? Perhaps there is. Burgess and Tawia point out that there are two types of experience: representational and sensational.[21] For the former, a functioning cortex seems to be a requisite property, for the latter however it is less certain that a functioning cortex is required. As Burgess and Tawia say, "sensation precedes conceptualised thought and consciously object-directed feelings and emotions".[22] Perhaps then, it is the case that the cortex provides the biological foundation of the conceptual, whilst the thalamus provides the foundation of the sensory. If the foetal experiences the two sides of the debate are focusing on can be represented in these terms, the apparent conflict could be explained.

Fitzgerald, as one of the main proponents of the debate discusses this issue within the context of the differing meanings of "experience" when she examines the notion of pain in the unborn foetus. There are two types of pain, she says, physiological which is instantaneous, and pathological with is ongoing.[23] By physiological pain Fitzgerald means the pure sensation of pain. For instance, placing one's hand in boiling water would result in physiological pain, the noxious stimulus would provoke an immediate physical reflex reaction resulting in withdrawal from the painful stimulus. Physiological pain would be an instance of that which Burgess and Tawia labelled sensational experience.[24]

Pathological pain, on the other hand, is described by Fitzgerald as "an ongoing consciously thought about pain". Pathological pain is not merely

---

[20] Noonan, *op.cit.* p. 211.
[21] Burgess and Tawia, *op. cit.*
[22] *Ibid.* p.5.
[23] See Fitzgerald *op. cit.*
[24] Burgess and Tawia, *op. cit.*

physical sensation, it is also an emotional experience that can be eased or heightened by memories of past experiences and associations. The pain associated with post-operative healing could be one such instance. Unlike physiological pain, this form of pain is experienced differently by different individuals, and is greatly affected by the individual's expectations, experiences, and knowledge. Pathological pain would be an example of the representational experience discussed by Burgess and Tawia. Pathological pain seemingly requires memory of past experiences and could not therefore be attributed to a pre-24-week-old foetus.

To move from this specific point to the claim that foetuses do not experience pain at all is, however, misleading. For, physiological pain may well require neither memory nor emotion to be experienced. As Glover and Fisk point out, "even if the nature of the experience changes with development this does not prove that immature humans cannot be distressed by pain".[25] Indeed, as Fitzgerald acknowledges, the physical stress responses associated in adults with physiological pain are evident in a foetus from as early as 16 weeks, and these physical responses can be reduced by the administering of analgesics. Fitzgerald concludes from this that "there must be a form of sensory input at this stage of development that produces a kind of pain reaction that can be dampened by analgesics".[26] Interestingly, analgesics do not work at the cortical level, they work at the thalamic level. And, if the thalamus is significant in the dampening of pain reactions that would be seen as significant in most non-human animals, it would seem reasonable to conclude that it is significant in the sensing of painful stimuli in human foetuses too.

Fitzgerald does not appear to see any significance in the relationship between pain reactions and the thalamus, despite the fact that in other cases such reactions would be taken as support for the possibility that pain is being experienced. For Fitzgerald however, there is no significance in foetal pain reactions at this stage of development because there is not yet a functioning cortex with which the human foetus can consciously experience pain on an emotional level. And, given Fitzgerald's definition of pain and its relationship with emotional awareness, such a conclusion appears to be warranted. But, given Glover's understanding of

---

[25] Vivette Glover & Nicholas Fisk (1996) 'Commentary: We Don't know; better to err on the safe side from mid-gestation', p. 796 of *The British Medical Journal*, v.313, 28 September.

[26] Fitzgerald, *op.cit.*

consciousness as a sensory rather than emotional phenomenon such evidence is significant.

As a result of these differing interpretations of consciousness it seems that the only point on which there is widespread agreement is that a post-24-week-old foetus is likely to be conscious: its cortex is connected and functioning from this point in its development, and consequently from this time on a foetus is, in all probability, aware of its world on a psychological level. What this may mean in terms of interaction with the social world we will investigate shortly.

But first, we should look a little more closely at the pre-24-week-old foetus. Is it possible, as some theorists are claiming, that a foetus of this age, a foetus without a functioning cortex is conscious? If consciousness at this stage of development is taken to mean mere sentience, there appears to be an increasing amount of evidence to support this possibility. Foetuses as young as 12-14 weeks will respond adversely to noxious stimuli, and from 16 weeks onwards analgesics will decrease the measurable physiological responses to these stimuli. Numerous examples of such behaviours have been documented, and Fitzgerald does not dispute these findings. It is only the meaning that ought to be attributed to them that is questioned.

According to Noonan, "beginning with the presence of sense receptors and spinal responses, there is as much reason to believe that the unborn are capable of pain as they are capable of sensation".[27] And, although unequivocal proof that the pre-24-week-old foetus is experiencing pain even on a sensory level cannot be presented, by applying the same reasoning as we do in the case of non-human animals, it would, as Liley says, seem reasonable to assume from their responses that they are.[28]

A second, and much stronger claim than mere sentience though, is that "many functions that were originally assumed to belong exclusively to the cortex can be undertaken by lower centres".[29] If this were so, then it could be the case that the pre-24-week-old foetus is conscious not only on a sensory level but also on a psychological level. There is some evidence to

---

[27] Noonan, *op.cit.* p. 311.
[28] Liley, *op.cit.* p. 32. As will be discussed in more detail in Chapter Seven, such responses are indeed taken as evidence of pain and suffering in non-human animals, as well as in human adults and children that cannot verbally communicate pain or suffering to their carers.
[29] 'Foetal Sentience: A Report by the All Party Parliamentary Pro-life Group' (1996) in *Catholic Medical Quarterly* XLVII, no.2, Nov.

support this claim. For instance, anencephalic and hydracephalic infants with relatively intact brain stems have been shown to exhibit "a surprising repertory of complex behaviours, including distinguishing their mother's voice from others, consolability, conditioning and associative learning...".[30] Lorber discusses one such case, in which a reduction of the thickness of the cerebral hemispheres (normally about 45 millimetres) to one millimetre or so occurred in an otherwise normal university student.[31] As Lorber notes, such evidence suggests that "...the cortex is probably responsible for a great deal less than most people imagine, many assumed cortical functions in this person were located in deep brain structures unaffected by hydrocephalus".[32]

Adult brain injury and stroke victims, who despite serious damage to their cortex can still experience some sensations with functioning lower areas in their brain, provide further support for such a possibility.[33] Support may also be found in pathological investigations such as the autopsy performed on Karen Ann Quinlan. Following the autopsy of Quinlan, it was concluded that:

> Although the neuropathological findings in Quinlan's case were multi-focal and complex, the disproportionately severe and bilateral damage in the thalamus as compared with damage in the cerebral cortex supports the hypothesis that the thalamus is critical for cognition and awareness and may be less central for arousal...[34]

---

[30] *Ibid.* See also 'The Problem of Pain: A Report by the Commission of Inquiry into Foetal Sentience', *op.cit.*

[31] Lorber, J. (1965) 'Hydraencephaly with normal development', pp. 628-633 of *Developmental Medicine and Child Neurology* 7. Though relatively dated, Lorber's discussion and conclusions in this article are still widely accepted today.

[32] *Ibid.* Lorber is not claiming that the lower areas of the brain can undertake all the functions of the cortex found in a normal adult. Rather, he is saying that the human brain develops in a "bottom-up" fashion, during which time the functions required are carried out by the structures present, and that as development progresses, some functions are taken over by higher areas of the brain. It is his opinion that this is a one-way transferral, and that the process cannot be reversed in the event of subsequent damage to the higher brain.

[33] 'Foetal Sentience: A Report by the All Party Parliamentary Pro-life Group', *op.cit.*

[34] Hannah C. Kinney et al. (1994) 'Neuropathological Findings in the Brain of Karen Ann Quinlan', pp. 1469-1475 of *The New England Journal of Medicine*, v.330 (21), May.

Unfortunately, the gradually accumulating body of evidence we have can so far only tell us that we do not yet have definitive answers to the question of foetal consciousness. To what degree a pre-24-week-old foetus is conscious is therefore not yet possible to determine with any degree of accuracy given our current level of knowledge.

However, the behavioural evidence that is slowly being amassed as technology increases our ability to study the early foetus in its natural environment, suggests that the 20-24 week old foetus is highly unlikely to be, as some claim, a totally insensate being, and that the 12-20 week old foetus may also be sentient to some degree. The unknown factor at this point in time, is the actual role the thalamus plays in the foetal brain. Until we learn more of this facet of foetal neurology, it is possible only to draw tentative conclusions. What does seem clear though, is that we ought to be wary of basing any firm conclusions in regards to the early foetal nervous system on what we know of the mature, healthy nervous system and the function of its components. As was noted during the Inquiry into Foetal Sentience, a foetus will respond to touch apparently prior to the arrival of the receptors responsible for tactile stimulation in adults (see Table 1: at 9 weeks a foetus's hands will respond when touched, yet the known sensory receptors are not in place until 2 weeks after that).

Given knowledge such as this, there are clearly factors at work that we, as yet, do not fully understand. Consequently, the most appropriate conclusion to be drawn in regards to a pre-24-week-old foetus, is that while it is probably not conscious: that is to say that it is probably not psychologically aware of and able to interact with its environment, the pre-24-week-old human foetus may well be sensate.

4 Active Potential and Foetal Psychology

Even if a post-24-week-old foetus is conscious though, what significance does this have for the debate over the nature and significance of its potential? As we have seen, to have an active potential to become a person the human foetus would need to manifest all of the morally significant positive causal factors necessary for the development of personhood: that is, it would need to possess a species-typical genetic structure, it would need to be sentient, conscious, and possess a capacity to interact with the social world. Prior to 24 weeks of development we know that a human foetus does not manifest all of these properties; it may possess a genetic structure sufficient to enable it to become conscious, but it is not yet sufficiently mature enough to actually do so. Even if the pre-24-week-old foetus is sentient as Glover and Fisk argue, it is not yet conscious: it does not yet have the capacity to consciously perceive and interact with the social world, consequently it cannot become self-aware, and cannot develop into a person. Thus, a pre-24-week-old foetus cannot possess an active potential to become a person.[1]

What can we say of the post-24-week-old foetus though? It seems to be consistently agreed upon that it is conscious, but is it social: does it have a manifest capacity to interact with, and learn from the social world?[2] This

---

[1] Whilst a sentient but not social foetus cannot have an active potential to become a person, and therefore cannot have a right to continued existence as a result of its potential, sentience is sufficient to grant a foetus a moral status that it does not possess prior to that point in its development. As a sentient being the foetus at this stage of development may well be able to experience pain, as such it may well have an interest in not being caused pain. This is an issue we will come back to in Chapter Seven when we look more closely at the rights of the foetus, and how it ought to be treated as a result of those rights.

[2] To ask whether a foetus can interact with the social world is to ask more than whether it can perceive and respond to physical states of affairs. There is no doubt that so far as the

may seem, on first glance, a foolish question. Clearly, a foetus at this age is normally *in utero*; it cannot see or touch those around it, so how can it possibly interact with the social world? It should be remembered, however, that what we are concerned with here is the presence of the capacity for social interaction, rather than actual on-going interaction. This is so because it is the capacity *per se* not the continual exercise of that capacity that is of moral consequence.

Evidently, the only way to determine whether such a capacity is present or not is to look for empirical evidence of its existence. But, as Hepper pointed out, in looking for this evidence it must be remembered:

> ...that a foetus lives in a very different environment from neonates, infants and adults. Consequently the abilities of the foetus will be tailored to his environment.... If this is not done [if the difference in environment is not acknowledged during investigations into foetal abilities] fetal abilities will be underestimated, and errors made regarding neonatal capabilities.[3]

As a result of the environmental restrictions, evidence of actual social interaction will necessarily be limited. Such limitations should not, however, be confused with a lack of capacity. For as will become clear there is a considerable degree of evidence to suggest that the post-24-week-old foetus has a manifest capacity to interact with other humans despite the fact that such interaction is physically restricted.

There is, a growing body of research centred around a foetus's ability to learn and remember whilst still *in utero*, which is thought by a wide variety of theorists to be a reflection of a much greater degree of cognitive ability than has been believed to be the case in the past.[4] It is no longer assumed, as was commonly accepted in past eras, that the human foetus is merely a

---

foetus's immediate physical surroundings are concerned: that is, the mother's womb, the amniotic fluid, the umbilical cord and so on, the foetus does interact on a regular basis. Of more interest is whether the unborn has the capacity to perceive stimuli that originate in other persons, and whether it can consciously respond to such stimuli.

[3] P.G. Hepper (1992) 'Foetal psychology: an embryonic science', pp. 129-156 of Nijhuis, J. *op.cit.* p. 132.

[4] Examples of the arguments of these theorists can be found in, 'The Problem of Pain: A Report by the Commission of Inquiry into Foetal Sentience', *op.cit.*; Tiffany M. Field and Nathan A. Fox (ed) (1985) *Social Perception in Infants*, Ablex Publishing Corporation, New Jersey; and Kenneth Kay, (1982) *The Mental and Social Life of Babies*, University of Chicago Press, Chicago.

passive being, oblivious to its surroundings. Past theorists may have discussed the human foetus and neonate in terms of a *"tabula rasa"* on which all future knowledge and experience is yet to be written; and as a "radical egocentric", meaning that the neonate is simply a "bundle of reflexes"; but today's theorists readily accept that the neonate is much more complex than this. The human neonate, as Meltzoff points out, "...does not simply have more reflexes, quicker reflexes, or more finely tuned sensory channels [than was assumed in the past] (although this may be true too). ...he is a very different kind of creature altogether".[5]

So, what are the actual psychological capacities of the foetus? What capacities does it possess, and could those capacities enable it to interact with and learn from the social world? We will begin an examination of these issues with a look at the purely sensory capacities of the human foetus. On a sensory level evidence is available to support foetal experience in the auditory, chemosensory, cutaneous and visual realms.[6]

The amniotic fluid is a good conductor of sound waves originating outside of the uterine walls, and foetal responses to sound have been reported from as early as 12 weeks.[7] Such responses are erratic however, and more consistent responses are not reported until much later in pregnancy. As Hepper and Shahidullah continue, "auditory stimulus elicits a reliable response from 28 weeks post-conception... whilst a change in [foetal] movements is observed from as early as 20 weeks.[8] These results are consistent with a positioning of the onset of foetal consciousness at around 24 weeks post-conception.

Taste and smell, as inter-related functions, cannot be differentiated from each other in the foetus due to its environment. However, many theorists have reported responses to chemosensory stimuli in utero. It is well documented, for instance, that a foetus can, from an early age, distinguish between sweetness and sourness (either by taste or smell), and that it has a

---

[5] Andrew N. Meltzoff, 'The Roots of Social and Cognitive Development: Models of Man's Original Nature', pp. 1-30 of Field & Nathan, *ibid.* p.24.
[6] Hepper, Peter G. and Shahidullah, Sara. (1994) 'The beginnings of mind – evidence from the behaviour of the foetus', pp. 143-154 of *Journal of Reproductive and Infant Psychology*, v.12.
[7] *Ibid.*
[8] *Ibid.* p. 146. See also R. Gagnon (1989) 'Stimulation of human foetuses with sound and vibration', pp. 393-402 of *Seminars in Perinatology*, v.13; and S. Shahidullah and P.G. Hepper (1993) 'The developmental origins of foetal responsiveness to an acoustic stimulus', pp. 135-142 of *Journal of Reproductive and Infant Psychology*, v.11.

36 *Interests in Abortion*

distinct preference for sweet things. Liley's observance of a clear increase in swallowing in response to saccharin being added to the amniotic fluid, and a corresponding decrease in the amount of swallowing in response to iodinated poppy seed oil being added to the amniotic fluid, is still being regularly replicated today.[9] The visual sense, as Hepper says, "...is probably the most unlikely to be stimulated during the normal course of pregnancy", however, responses to experimental light stimuli have been recorded *in utero* from 26 weeks post-conception.[10] Once again this data is consistent with the claims made in the previous chapter concerning the beginnings of foetal consciousness.

The functioning of the final sense (touch) appears to be somewhat more problematic. Perhaps this is partially because of the implications a functioning tactile system in the foetus could have for the currently accepted treatment of human foetuses. Nevertheless, there are many reports of foetal responses to tactile stimulation at almost every point throughout its development. And, whilst this issue will be considered in some detail at a later point, it is useful to note here that the foetus first responds to touch at eight weeks when a reflex response is elicited by the touching of its upper lip. Its responsiveness to touch then steadily increases, until by 14 weeks post-conception a human foetus will respond to touch on every part of its body except its back and the top of its head.[11]

Of these sensory capacities, which, if any, could contribute to an unborn foetus's capacity to interact with the social world though? On a minimal level perhaps it could be claimed that all of a foetus's sensory abilities contribute to this process. If a foetus begins to develop taste preferences prior to birth, if its sleep-wake cycles begin to adapt in response to the light that permeates the walls of the womb, and if it responds to the position the mother is sitting or lying in either favourably or unfavourably, surely all of these senses are enabling it to interact with the world it is yet to be born into. We must, however, be careful to differentiate between a foetus's ability to respond to its immediate physical environment, and its ability to respond to more significant external stimuli that originates in

---

[9] See A.W. Liley (1972) 'The foetus as a personality', pp. 99-105 of *Australian and New Zealand Journal of Psychiatry*, v.6, cited in Hepper and Shahidullah, *ibid.*

[10] Hepper and Shahidullah, *ibid.* and D. Peleg, and J.A. Goldman (1980) 'Foetal heart rate acceleration in response to light stimulation as a clinical measure of foetal well-being: a preliminary report', pp. 38-41 of *Journal of Perinatal Medicine* v.8.

[11] Hepper and Shahidullah, *ibid.*

human action. Consequently, despite empirical findings of sensory functioning one must be careful not to draw unwarranted conclusions. "Whilst there is little doubt", as Hepper and Shahidullah say, "that the foetus senses its environment whether it perceives it [on a conscious level] is unknown".[12] Having said this, it should also be noted that with our as yet incomplete knowledge, the absence of response from a particular sense should not lead us to the conclusion that that sense is neither present nor functioning. For, as Hepper and Shahidullah continue, it is also possible that "...the foetus may have an immature motor system, such that although the foetus senses the stimulus it is unable to respond".[13]

Foetal Learning

Is our knowledge as incomplete as such conclusions appear to say though? If, in addition to looking at foetal sensory responses throughout pregnancy, we also examine the nature of foetal learning, a less uncertain, more holistic picture of foetal capacities begins to emerge. There is a significant and growing body of evidence to support the claim that the human foetus, at least in its final months of development, is not merely physically sensing stimuli in ways such as those discussed above, but that it is also perceiving external stimuli on a conscious level.

Piaget, a foundational learning theorist, "...has always argued that structures are constructed over time and that complex coordinated systems must evolve...no structures can appear full-blown out of nothing".[14] Following this line of thought, it would appear to be evident that any complex psychological capacities manifest in a newborn infant must have been preceded by less complex evolving abilities. And, given the complexity of a newborn's behavioural repertoire there is good reason to suppose that the human foetus is not only sensate but also conscious at some point prior to its birth. To examine this issue we will begin by looking at the evidence for pre-natal learning gained from studies of both pre- and post-birth infants. We will then move on to examine just what

---

[12] *Ibid.* p. 147.
[13] *Ibid.*
[14] Wanda Franz (1981) 'Foetal Development: A novel Application of Piaget's Theory of Cognitive Development', pp. 36-44 of Thomas Hilgers *et al.*, *New Perspectives on Human Abortion*, Aletheia Books, Maryland. *op.cit.*

complex abilities the neonate possesses, and finally we will address the question of what more fundamental cognitive abilities may have preceded the neonatal abilities that could provide evidence of pre-natal consciousness?

Cognition, as Goswami defined it, is "...the set of processes that enable us to gain information about our environments – processes such as learning, memory, reasoning and problem solving".[15] While it is not being claimed here that the human foetus or neonate is capable of reasoning or problem solving, it is being suggested that their memory and learning abilities are sufficiently developed by full term to ground rudimentary social interaction. It will further be claimed that the capacity for social interaction evident in the full term neonate must also be present during the final stages of *in utero* development.

There are numerous examples of a foetus's capacity to learn from its external environment both by habituation and by classical conditioning. Evidence of the capacity to learn in these ways has been found from as early as 22-23 weeks of development in the case of habituation, and from 30-32 weeks in the case of classical conditioning.[16] Such behaviours can only be explained as a result of the unborn infant responding to, and adapting to the world outside of its immediate uterine environment. One of the most overt recorded examples of this is the behaviour of infants that live near Osaka airport in Japan (one of the world's busiest airports). In studying the behaviour of these infants, it was found that if a woman moved to a housing estate close to the runway prior to six and a half months gestation, the newborn would only wake up 5% of the time when a jet took off. But, if the mother moved to the same area after seven months gestation, the infant would wake up 55% of the time.[17] Such clear results show not only that human foetuses can adapt to occurrences outside of their immediate environment, but that they begin to do so at an early age (26-28 weeks in this instance). Similar examples of classical conditioning have also been abundant in recent years.[18]

---

[15] Usha Goswami (1998) *Cognition in Children*, Psychology Press, London.
[16] *Ibid*.
[17] Marshall H. Klaus and Phyllis Klaus (1985) *The Amazing Newborn*, Addison-Wesley Publishing, Massachusetts, pp. 136-138.
[18] See, for instance, Peter G. Hepper (1991) 'An examination of foetal learning before and after birth', pp. 95-107 of *Irish Journal of Psychology*, v.12(2); and L.P. Lipsett (1990)

But, some could respond, habituation and classical conditioning are learning behaviours evident in a wide variety of animal species, and as such they are certainly not indicative of a potential for personhood. Why then, should they be taken as evidence in the human foetus? The answer is that alone they would not be taken as such, but as two parts of a much larger body of evidence they do provide support for the claim that at some point after 24 weeks post-conception the human foetus has a manifest capacity to perceive and respond to the extrauterine environment. And this, as was discussed earlier, is the central issue: not whether there is evidence of complex social relationships being formed prior to the foetus's birth – clearly there is not – but whether the unborn human foetus has the capacity to participate in, and learn from, the social world. For it is this capacity that must necessarily be present if the foetus is to possess an active potential to become a person.

"In order to learn", as Hepper pointed out, "the foetus must be able to perceive the stimulus and must also retain some form of memory of it in order for recognition to be exhibited after birth".[19] In the process of testing this hypothesis, a relatively new body of information concerning more complex forms of learning has begun to develop. First and foremost in the continuing dialogue that the foetus hears prior to its birth is, of course, its mother's voice. As a result of this exposure the newborn infant is clearly able to differentiate between its mother's and other female voices.[20] When given a choice between their mother's voice and that of a female stranger newborns clearly show a preference for the voice of their mother. And, when given a choice between their mother's voice as it sounded whilst they were still *in utero* and their mother's voice as it sounds from outside the womb, newborns clearly prefer that which sounds as it did prior to their birth.[21] These results indicate that the preferences shown by neonates in regards to their mother's voice are acquired prenatally.[22]

'Learning processes in the human newborn', pp. 113-127 of *Annals of New York Academy of Sciences*, v.608.

[19] Hepper and Shahidullah *op.cit.* p. 150.

[20] A.J. DeCasper and M.J. Spence (1986) 'Prenatal maternal speech influences newborn's perception of speech sounds', pp. 133-150 of *Infant Behaviour and Development*, v.9.

[21] W.P. Fifer and C. Moon (1989) 'Psychobiology of new-born auditory preferences', pp. 430-433 of *Seminars in Perinatology*, v.13.

[22] Peter G. Hepper and Sara Shahidullah, *op.cit.*

More than just the mother's voice is learnt by the foetus and remembered by the neonate however. Four-day-old infants will suck harder to hear their parent's native language than they do to hear a foreign language, and infants can apparently detect differences between the phonemes in those languages.[23] Another experiment, reported by Kolata, illustrated that newborn infants prefer stories that had been read to them before birth, over similar sounding but unfamiliar stories. The newborn infants of women who read *The Cat in the Hat* aloud twice a day for six and a half weeks before birth, showed a clear tendency to adopt a sucking pattern that allowed them to hear that same story, rather than another similarly rhymed one also read by the mother.[24] Hepper, in a similar vein, found that newborn infants apparently recognised the theme tune of a popular television program that they had heard regularly prior to birth, and that their preference for that tune over others lasted for approximately three weeks after birth.[25] Each of these, and many more experiments, give support to the proposition that the unborn foetus both perceives its environment on an auditory level, and that it remembers its experiences after birth.

But, some may still ask, how can these behaviours be clearly differentiated from the learning behaviours of lower animals such as fish, which clearly have both a capacity to habituate to stimuli, and a capacity to be conditioned? Perhaps the form of memory, which is being utilised by the human foetus and neonate, is of the same unconscious form as that utilised by the lower animals? The best way to answer these questions is to examine one such learning experiment in more detail. For this purpose we will focus on Goswami's report of DeCasper and Fifer's 1980 research.[26]

> DeCasper and Fifer first measured how strongly infants sucked on a dummy in the absence of any auditory stimulus [in order to determine a baseline measurement]. They then introduced two tape recordings, one of the infant's

---

[23] See J. Mehler, et al. (1998) 'A precursor to language development in young infants', pp. 143-178 of *Cognition*, v.29; and G. Dehaene-Lambertz and S. Denaene (1994) 'Speed and cerebral correlates of syllable discrimination in infants', pp. 292-294 of *Nature*, v.37, both of which are discussed by Eisenberg, *op.cit.*

[24] Gina Kolata (1984) 'Studying learning in the womb', pp. 302-304 of *Science*, v.225, July 20.

[25] Hepper (1991) *op.cit.*

[26] A.J. DeCasper and W.P. Fifer, 'Of human binding: newborns prefer their mother's voices', pp. 1174-1176 of *Science*, 1980, v.208.

mother reading a story, and one of a strange woman reading the same story. For some infants every time their suck rate increased compared to baseline, they were rewarded with the tape of their mother's voice. Every time their suck rate fell below the baseline measure, they heard the tape of the voice of the stranger. For other infants, the contingencies were reversed...
Both groups of infants rapidly learned to suck at the appropriate rate to hear their mother's voice. This shows that they remembered the sound of their own mother's voice, and that it was a familiar and comforting stimulus. Even more impressive, they could remember the contingency in a second test session given on the following day. Babies who had learned to suck strongly to hear their mother began by sucking strongly on the dummy, and those who had learned to suck slowly began by sucking slowly. The experimenters, however, had reversed the contingencies. Babies who had learned to suck strongly for their mother's voice were now meant to suck slowly and babies who had learned to suck slowly were now meant to suck strongly. Around 80% of the babies learned to reverse their suck rate. This is good evidence for learning and memory in these extremely young babies. In fact, the ability to reverse a learned rule is considered to be a strong test of cognition in animals, and so the rapid learning found in these babies shows that day-old babies are at least as cognitively sophisticated as rats and pigeons, and more cognitively sophisticated than goldfish, who cannot learn the rule reversals even after thousands of trials![27]

Thus, to answer the question, how do we know that human neonates' learning abilities and memory are any more complex than those of lower non-conscious animals? Research such as that DeCasper and Fifer's amply illustrates that it is, for in some cases the complexity of the actions required of the infants is such that it must consciously attend to the stimulus if it is to learn the required behavioural response.

Furthermore, it is possible to extrapolate from the data obtained in experimental situations concerning the psychological capacities of day old infants, to the psychological capacities of full term unborn foetuses. Given that a neonate is considered to be full term even if it is born several days prior to its due date, it seems reasonable to conclude that the measurable psychological capacities of the neonate are also present in as yet unborn full-term foetuses.

There are three further neonatal capacities that strongly suggest that the newborn infant already possesses a capacity to interact with the social

---

[27] Goswami, *op cit.* p.2.

world. These are interactional synchrony, imitation, and turn-taking. These three behaviours appear to show not only that the human neonate has a preference for human interaction over all other forms of interaction and that it is an active participant in the process of human interaction, but that it can discriminate between human and non-human attempts at interaction.

The first of these behaviours, interactional synchrony, concerns the newborn infant's apparently innate ability to time its bodily movements with the pattern of the human voice. Bower describes interactional synchrony as "...a form of motor behaviour seen whenever one human speaks to another. Both speaker and listener move together... the moves being made in precise synchrony with the segments of the speaker's speech".[28] The movements of the participants are usually very small and are generally not observed by the naked eye, but they are consistently observed and recorded by time-frame photography in infants only hours after birth.[29]

The second social behaviour that is apparent in human infants is imitation. Newborn infants will imitate the facial expressions (and perhaps the body movements) of other humans when interacting with them on a one-to-one basis.[30] Followers of Piaget have traditionally seen this behaviour as one requiring an "elaborate cognitive structure" before it can be manifested.[31] Such a claim would seem unlikely to be correct however, as imitation has been recorded by many theorists in the very first hours and

---

[28] T.G.R. Bower (1974) *Development in Infancy*, WH Freeman and Company, San Francisco, p.256. See also Hepper and Shahidullah, *op.cit.*

[29] *Ibid.*

[30] *Ibid.* See also A. Vintner (1986) 'The role of movement in eliciting early imitations', pp. 66-71 of *Child Development*, 57.

[31] The rationale behind Piaget's claims regarding the complexity of this behaviour concerns the possibility of the imitator (the neonate in this instance) having to be able to discriminate between its different body parts, and between itself and others. Imitating facial expressions is a complex task, requiring the infant to be able to relate the observed movements with its own body parts. To open its mouth, widen its eyes, open its hands, or stick its tongue out in response to another doing so, the infant must first be able to associate that movement with its own body parts, and secondly it must be able to make the corresponding movement without being able to see its own body. This, it has been claimed, requires some form of abstract or conceptual thought. The possibility will not be developed here. It is an intriguing possibility though, that has led some theorists to postulate that the newborn infant has both a generalised concept of self, and a concept of others.

days after birth of both term and pre-term neonates.[32] It is interesting to note here that whilst pre-term infants with an average age of 34.5 weeks were found to be as capable of imitation as their full-term counterparts, the behaviour was shorter-lived and slightly less frequently recorded in the case of the pre-term infants. This, it is suggested, is indicative of two things: firstly, that foetuses prior to full term possess a capacity to imitate other humans, and secondly, that the attentional processes of the neonate develop more slowly than the imitative capacities.[33]

A similar result was found in studies of voice and facial discrimination. It is, as Fields points out, generally accepted that infants perceive social stimuli such as faces and voices more readily than other visual and auditory stimuli.[34] What is not so often discussed is the degree of discrimination within the infant's perception of human faces and voices. Spence and DeCasper, for instance, showed that there is a marked preference for the mother's voice and face, even in very young neonates. And, as Field says:

> Preference for the mother's face in the initial recognition test is remarkable, particularly given that the neonates had only experienced four discontinuous hours with the mother prior to participation in the study. The preference for mothers' faces suggests that despite limited exposure to their mother these newborns discriminated at least some aspect of the mother's face.[35]

The ability to discriminate was, once again, found not only in full term infants but also in preterm neonates with an average age gestational age of 34.5 weeks (although the development of this ability is, as Fields notes, "more marked in full term infants").[36]

One other neonatal behaviour that provides evidence of social conduct is turn-taking. Kozack Mayer and Tronick point out that "Just as language has lexical, syntactical and semantic rules which govern acceptable and unacceptable linguistic acts, so too, face-to-face interaction is comprised of

---

[32] *Ibid.* Interestingly, both interactional synchrony and imitation can apparently be elicited only by other human voices and faces, no other stimuli, mechanical or animal, will evoke them.
[33] Vintner, *op.cit.*
[34] Tiffany Field, 'Neonatal perception of people and individual differences', pp. 31-52 of Field and Fox, *op.cit.*
[35] *Ibid.*
[36] *Ibid.*

acts with acceptable and unacceptable options".[37] Turn-taking is one such rule. In the numerous experiments that have focused on mother-infant interaction it has been convincingly shown, as Kozak and Tronick illustrate, that "although the infant is not yet conversational in the sense of engaging in an exchange of content, the infant is conversational in having mastered the rudiments of the basic form of human interchange".[38]

But are the behaviours discussed above evidence of social interaction? Yes, according to Bower's definition of social behaviour, they are. Bower says that "social behaviour is behaviour that is not terminated by delivery of food, drink, warmth, or comfort...[and] one that is elicited by the presence of another human and terminated by the departure of that human".[39] In the cases discussed above, each of the responses of the infant are distinct from its physical needs; they are either a direct consequence of the infant's memory of experiences had prior to its birth, or a result of interaction with other humans in the days immediately following its birth; they are elicited by the actions of another human, and terminated by the departure of that human. Consequently, interactional synchrony, imitation, and turn-taking are unequivocally social behaviours by Bower's definition.

These behaviours, along with memory of its mother's voice, an ability to learn the speech patterns of its mother, and the rhythmic sounds of stories that are told to it, are all evidence of specifically human modes of interaction. And, the presence of a manifest capacity to perceive these stimuli prior to birth is illustrated by the newborn infant's reaction to these stimuli following birth. If an infant can learn to act according to preferences developed prior to its birth, if it can remember specific sounds and voices heard prior to birth, if it can discriminate between those sounds and voices and others heard subsequent to its birth, then the human foetus prior to birth must be interacting with the social world. If one adds to these capacities the manifest social behaviours of full-term and pre-term infants discussed above there would seem to be little doubt that the unborn human foetus has the psychological capacity to interact with the social world, and that to a limited extent it is exercising that capacity prior to its birth. As Field says:

---

[37] Nancy Kozak Mayer and Edward Z. Tronick, 'Mother's turn-giving signals and Infant turn-taking in mother-infant interaction', pp. 199-216 of Field and Fox *op.cit.* p. 199.
[38] *Ibid.*
[39] Bower, *op.cit.* p. 256.

It appears that even the youngest infant is not an asocial creature in a state anything akin to the "normal autism" or "radical egocentrism" that has been attributed to them in the past...young infants, even newborns, can recognise human acts as like their own, and have a rich set of tools for building further bridges between themselves and others.[40]

A Potential Person

What does this mean in terms of foetal potential? We saw at the beginning of this chapter that to possess an active potential to become a person, a foetus must possess all of the positive causal factors required for personhood, and that it must have no negative causal factors to block the operation of the positive ones. We also saw that to have all of the positive causal factors required for personhood, a human foetus had to have an appropriate genetic structure, it had to manifest sentience and consciousness, and it had to have a manifest capacity to interact with its social world. On investigating the physiological and psychological properties of the foetus we determined that the physiological properties required for the manifestation of the necessary psychological properties are present in the human foetus by 24 weeks of development, and that the required psychological capacities become manifest at some point between then and 38 weeks, or full-term.

Commonly accepted learning theory developed by Piaget rests on the assumption that cognitive skills are cumulative: the manifestation of complex learning structures is dependent on the exercise of less complex structures. If infants only hours old can attend to stimuli and consciously adapt their behaviour to achieve a desired response, then a full term foetus must also possess this ability. And, if full-term foetuses possess this skill, the younger foetus must, at a minimum, possess a more rudimentary psychological capacity in which this capacity is grounded. Given the evidence discussed above it seems likely that psychological awareness precedes attentiveness. As such, it is plausible to conclude that the unborn foetus is, at some stage, psychologically aware of its environment, though not yet able to consciously attend to specific stimuli, or direct its behaviour to achieve a desired response.

---

[40] Field, *op.cit.* p. 27.

At what stage a psychological awareness first arises though, cannot yet be determined with any degree of accuracy. We know that a biological capacity for consciousness is present at 24 weeks post-conception, at which time the connections between the higher and lower centres of the brain are firmly established. We also know that at around this point in time predictable sensory responses are obtained; that memory on some level is both present and functioning; and that by 34-38 weeks post-conception memory, the ability to consciously attend to stimuli and act so as to achieve a desired response are all evident. We know, therefore, that at some point in time between 24 weeks and 38 weeks post-conception a human foetus becomes conscious: it comes to be aware of its environment not merely at a sensory level, but also on a psychological level.

More than this is evident by the end of this period however. By 34-38 weeks post-conception the many studies of foetal and neonatal behaviour show that the foetus/infant has a manifest capacity to interact with, adapt to, remember, and learn from its existence in the social world. Thus, we know that the human foetus is at this time no longer an object existing passively within its environment, but a psychologically aware subject of experiences. The problem is in determining the exact point between 24 and 38 weeks of development a human foetus ceases to be a passive participant in its environment, and becomes an active subject of conscious experiences.

Indeed, it seems doubtful that there is an exact point in time in which this development occurs. Thus, with no more precise data than this available, it would seem that the only non-arbitrary point to advance as the beginning of the human subject is the point at which the connections between the cortex and the lower areas of the brain are firmly established, and the cortex begins to function. At this point in time, when the human foetus has manifested all of the morally significant positive causal factors of personhood, its potential to become a person is an active potential: it has within it all of the morally relevant positive causal factors required for personhood, and no negative factors within it to preclude the expression of the positive factors. At this point in time, the identity relation between the human foetus and person it becomes will no longer be merely a numerical identity: it will, as we will see in the next chapter, be a much more significant form of identity. From 24 weeks of development the human foetus, as a psychologically aware subject of experiences, is a morally relevant potential person.

5 Personal Identity and the Human Foetus

Parfit's Identity Criterion

What does it mean to say that something is a morally relevant potential person though? It is unproblematic to say that an actual person is a morally relevant being, but why should a *potential* person, a being that does not yet have the valued capacities of an actual person, be morally relevant? One plausible answer to this question revolves around the issue of identity. To put it very simply, an argument from potential generally amounts to the claim that a potential person and the actual person it becomes are the *very same being*, and that consequently the potential person already has within it something of great moral value, which will become manifest if the potential person continues its process of development. Of course, on one level, that of numerical identity, the foetus that is a potential person is obviously the very same being as the person it becomes. This truism, however, can tell us little of moral consequence. More important is whether there is another more significant sense in which the foetus and the person it becomes share their identity. We will begin our investigation into this possibility with a look at a popular theory of identity. We will then go on to apply this theory of identity to the foetus and person it becomes, in order to determine whether there is a morally significant relationship between them; and whether that relationship is sufficient to grant the post-24-week-old foetus rights that are normally attributable only to actual persons.

There is a complex and ongoing debate over the nature and meaning of personal identity, and to enter into this debate would necessitate an entire book in its own right. Consequently, I will accept and employ Parfit's notion of identity throughout this discussion, as it is one of the most plausible and widely accepted explanations of identity that is currently in use.[1] In general, to claim that a being persists over time is to say that despite both external and internal changes, being X at t_1 is the very same being as being Y at t_2. A determination of the truth of this statement in specific circumstances is generally taken to be a determination of personal identity. Parfit says, however, that in order to determine whether X at t_1 is the very same being as person at t_2 one ought to be less concerned with trying to define personal identity *per se*, and more concerned with what he calls "Relation R": that is, one ought to be concerned with the presence or absence of "psychological connectedness and/or continuity, with the right kind of cause".[2] For, it is his claim that it is the presence of Relation R that is necessary for a being to persist over time.

Because we are searching for a form of continued identity between two beings – only one of which is an actual person, Parfit's conceptualisation of identity relations is particularly applicable to the question at hand. In cases in which either one of the beings in question is not an actual person the identity relation between them cannot logically be defined as personal identity. It would seem however, that, as a relationship of degrees, Relation R could exist between a human foetus and the person it becomes.[3] If it were the case that a strong version of Relation R existed between a human foetus at t_1 and the human person it became at t_2, one would seem compelled to conclude that the foetus was not merely a potential person, but an actual person: the very same actual person as the person at t_2. It is unlikely, however, that this is the case. If Relation R does, in fact, exist between a human foetus and the person it becomes, it is more probable that it is a weak version of Relation R – one that encompasses the factors necessary for the foetus and person to be the same subject of experience, but not to the degree required for the continuation of actual personhood

If this were found to be the case, the existence of a weak version of Relation R would support the claim that the post-24-week-old foetus and the person it becomes while not the same person, are one and the same enduring subject of experience. Before looking at this claim to see if it is sufficient to grant an increased moral status to the foetus, however, we

---

[1] See Derek Parfit *op.cit.*
[2] Parfit goes on to claim that the right kind of cause is "any kind of cause", so long as the relationship does not take a branching form such that the first being is said to be identical to two or more different future beings, *ibid.* p. 206.
[3] See Parfit, *ibid.*, and also Marvin Belzer (1996) 'Notes on Relation R', *Analysis* 56 (1), Jan.

must first look in some detail at exactly what is meant by Relation R, and what its presence would entail in a strong form and in a weak form.

What exactly does Parfit mean by Relation R: psychological continuity and/or connectedness with the right kind of cause? Memories are the most obvious psychological connection between a being's past and present selves. As More says, "being able to remember *from the inside* actions carried out by an earlier person, is perhaps the most fundamental aspect of our psychology that makes us aware of our own continued existence over time".[4] Despite their prominence however, memories alone are not sufficient to secure identity over time. Many theorists, including Parfit, have illustrated that one can quite plausibly hold memories of past actions yet be an essentially different person to the one that carried out those actions. If, for instance, one's character was altered, if one's desires, intentions, beliefs, and perhaps even gender were changed after the actions in question, it would be difficult to justify the claim that the person with the memories was the very same person as the one who originally acted. It follows from this that it is not just memory, but all of the above factors, that can play a part in a person's psychological connectedness and continuity over time.

Parfit would apparently agree with this analysis: "one direct psychological connection", he notes, "is not sufficient for identity, rather there must be a strong psychological connectedness" between the prior and later stages of the being in question, and strong connectedness only exists when there are "...*enough* direct psychological connections".[5] Which, Parfit goes on to explain, means that there must be "...at least half the number of direct psychological connections that hold over every day in the lives of nearly every actual person".[6] Such a degree of connectedness can, as we noted above, be constituted by many different psychological components. For instance, there would be a direct psychological connection between being Y at t_2 and being X at t_1 if the intentions of X at t_1 *directly* caused the actions of Y at t_2. Similarly, X at t_1 would be

---

[4] Max More (1995) *The Diachronic Self: Identity, Continuity and Transformation*, an unpublished doctoral dissertation which can be viewed at http://www.primnet.com/~maxmore/chapter1.htm.
[5] Parfit, *op.cit.*
[6] *Ibid.*

50 *Interests in Abortion*

psychologically connected to Y at t_2 if X's desires at t_1 directly affected the actions of Y at t_2.[7]

Though these and other factors do not constitute direct psychological connections as overtly as do memories, they can serve to tie the different stages of a person together across time by virtue of their being able to affect the actions the person undertakes in the future, and the manner in which those actions are carried out. X's dispositions at t_1, for example, can not only lead to predictable responses at later times, they can also lead to the development of new beliefs, habits and desires. Each of which may in turn have an effect on X's future actions. Even though the new beliefs, desires and so on may be distinct, perhaps even diametrically opposed to X's beliefs and desires at t_1, the original disposition that helped shape them would nevertheless provide a direct psychological connection between X's past and future psychological states.

In cases in which there are enough such direct connections in a person's psychology over time to constitute strong connectedness, and in cases in which these connections overlap in time (as the links in a chain overlap in space) psychological continuity would also exist.[8] And, as the person at t_1 and the person at t_2 would then share psychological connectedness and/or continuity, Relation R would exist between them, and those two persons would be identical – they would be the very same being.

Relation R and the Human Foetus

Given this understanding of a being's continuation over time, we can now return to our discussion of the human foetus's relationship to the person it will become. The post-24-week-old foetus, as we saw in the previous chapter, is conscious, it can interact with the social world (albeit in a limited fashion given its environment), and it can learn from that interaction. Is it plausible to maintain that it shares the strong version of Relation R pointed to by Parfit, with the person it becomes, and that it is therefore identical to the person it will become? No, for by definition if a

---

[7] See More *op.cit.* for a fuller discussion of the relative importance of each of these, and other factors, to the overall degree of psychological connectedness of two or more selves.

[8] In Parfit's words, "overlapping chains of strong connectedness" constitute psychological continuity, *op.cit.*

foetus is identical to the person it becomes it too must be a person. But, as we will see, there clearly are both direct psychological connections between the foetus and the infant it becomes, and a form of psychological continuity between the foetus and person it becomes. So what identity relation do the foetus and the person share? I will argue here that these factors are sufficient for the presence of a weak version of Relation R between the foetus and person, and that a shared weak version of Relation R entails that they are the very same subject of experience, even though they are not the very same person.

As we have seen in the previous chapter, there is a growing body of evidence to support the claim that the human infant remembers its pre-birth experiences. Studies showing that human neonates can recognise their mother's voice in comparison with other female voices;[9] experimental results showing newborn infants' apparent preferences for what would appear to be familiar vocal patterns and sounds that were experienced prior to birth;[10] and a growing number of case studies[11] all provide reason to suppose that the newborn infant is responding to memories of experiences had prior to birth. While not all of these memories are necessarily conscious experiences of the infant's *in utero* existence, some clearly do appear to be conscious.

The crucial point, however, is not whether the memories of the neonate are either all conscious or whether some are unconscious memories, but whether they directly cause or affect the experiences and behaviour of the neonate and person it becomes. As was seen earlier in this chapter memories alone do not constitute psychological connectedness from Parfit's perspective: other facets of psychology such as preferences, dispositions, desires, and behavioural patterns, are also components of Relation R. Looked at singularly the existence of each of these facets of a neonate's psychology may not provide strong support for the claim that there is a form of psychological connectedness between the neonate and the foetus it once was. Consequently, there would seem little reason to suppose that there is a form of psychological continuity between the foetus and person the neonate becomes. Looked at as elements of a whole,

---

[9] DeCasper and M.J. Spence, *op.cit.*
[10] See Mehler, *et al. op.cit.*, Dehaene-Lambertz and S Denaene, *op.cit.*; Kolata, *op.cit.*; and Hepper (1991) *op.cit.*
[11] See, for example, William B. Sallanbach (1994) 'Claira: A Case Study in Prenatal Learning, pp. 33-56 of *Pre- and Perinatal Psychology Journal*, 9(1), Fall.

however, there would seem to be little doubt that psychological connectedness does exist between the post-24-week-old foetus and the infant it becomes. In which case there is no reason to suppose that there is not a form of psychological continuity between the post-24-week-old foetus and the person the neonate becomes.

Apart from the evidence of neonatal memory that was discussed above, what other connections have been observed and recorded, one may ask. One example of such connections can be seen in Liley's work. Liley points out that certain unconscious neonatal "preferences" such as choice of sleeping position and feeding patterns apparently mirror those of the foetus prior to birth. In Liley's words:

> If newborn babies are nursed naked in a warm environment, they tend to adopt – especially when asleep – the position of comfort they assumed *in utero* in late pregnancy. Thus some babies sleep with their hands cupped under their ears, and the baby whose legs were extended *in utero* tends to sleep like a safety pin, with a foot over each shoulder.[12]

In a similar vein, he goes on to discuss the finding that "the fast drinkers *in utero* are the same in the nursery; the slow drinkers *in utero* are dainty, tedious feeders in the nursery".[13] The psychological connections between the foetus, infant, and person it becomes are currently under consideration by some in the psychiatric profession too. As Hepper points out, it may be the case that pre-birth experiences predispose the future person to develop certain personality traits. In his words, "Behaviour acquired in the womb would predispose the individual to respond in certain ways after birth. This would further reinforce inappropriate actions, and the cycle might continue and develop into a psychiatric disorder".[14]

Such a possibility was also hinted at by Fitzgerald, who despite her conclusions that the pre-24-week-old foetus is not a conscious or sentient being, cautions her audience against the possibility of causing permanent damage in the person the foetus becomes as a result of influencing the pain receptors of the unborn foetus. As she pointed out, "by introducing stimuli during foetal development, you are actually reprogramming the wiring,

---

[12] Liley, *op.cit.* p. 31.
[13] *Ibid.* p. 33.
[14] Peter Hepper (1989) 'Foetal Learning: Implications for Psychiatry', pp. 289-293 of *British Journal of Psychiatry*, 155. p. 292.

something that then carries forward into the rest of [its] life".[15] To put this another way, the neurological, physiological, and therefore psychological development of the person the foetus becomes could be affected by actions directed at the unborn foetus.

Purely on the basis of the large number of quantitative studies undertaken in the last two or three decades, such as those discussed in this and previous chapters, it would seem clear that there is a psychological connection between the post-24-week-old foetus and, at the very least, the infant it becomes. Another avenue of research that has not yet been examined but that also supports this thesis is qualitative research. There is a gradually developing body of qualitative research data being accumulated, that focuses on the psychological relationship between the foetus, infant and child it becomes.[16] Similar to the research discussed above, the results of these studies also appear to be indicative of a psychological connectedness between the foetus and the infant.

In one such study, that of Piontelli, it is claimed that there is "...a remarkable continuity in aspects of pre-natal and post-natal life. Each foetus [in the study] had characteristic ways of behaving which were, to some extent...continued in post-natal life".[17] A brief look at the methodology and results of this study will illustrate why this claim is being made. Piontelli undertook behavioural case studies of single foetuses, identical, and non-identical twins during their foetal, infantile, and early childhood development. Detailed recordings of the behavioural, and later the psychological development of each foetus from mid-gestation to birth were obtained via regular and prolonged ultrasound viewing, the progress of the infants and children was then followed for the next three years of their life.[18] It was found, as can be seen in the table below, that the

---

[15] See Maria Fitzgerald's evidence presented to the *Inquiry into Foetal Sentience, op.cit.* Fitzgerald is opposed to some of the ideas presented earlier in this paper concerning the psychological awareness of the unborn foetus, she does however acknowledge that if a foetus continues to develop into a person "painful stimulation [during foetal development] may well affect the fundamental development of the nervous system". As she states earlier in her discussion, "it [the foetus] might not be something that has an emotional response but it has a fundamental response to the rest of that infant's development".

[16] See, for instance, Sallanbach *op.cit.*; and Alessandra Piontelli (1992) *From Foetus to Child: an observational and psychoanalytic study*, Routledge, London.

[17] Piontelli, *ibid.* p. 1.

[18] The study is in fact continuing but the currently published results only cover this period.

54 *Interests in Abortion*

behaviours of the foetuses were largely carried through into the behavioural and psychological traits of the children they developed into.

Table 2: Results of Piontelli's Case Studies

Case No.	Type of Pregnancy	Behaviours Recorded *in utero*	Behaviours Recorded in Infancy & Childhood
1	Single foetus	Inactive, relaxed, often recorded via ultrasound licking placenta	Passive, quiet, sucking reflex not well established at birth, initially would only lick mother's breast
2	Single foetus	Active throughout the majority of pregnancy.	Active adventurous child
3	Non-identical twins[19]	Male less active than female, no interaction recorded between them	Male larger than female and overtly preferred by parents, but female much more outgoing and alert than male
4	Non-identical twins	Male and female, both quiet, relaxed, often appeared to be stroking each other	Both male and female quiet gentle children, who enjoyed each other's company and liked to be physically touching each other
5	Non-identical twins	Two females both active, often recorded apparently hitting each other.	Loud children, who continually fought with each other
6	Identical twins	Physically inter-twined during pregnancy	Appeared to intensely dislike each other but couldn't bear to be separated[20]

---

[19] *In utero* studies of twins and other multiple births provide some fascinating research opportunities. Their unique situation presents the opportunity to investigate the possibility of interaction prior to birth which has, prior to the development of ultrasound and *in utero* video recordings, not been possible. Such studies are beginning to accumulate as our technological ability to study the *in utero* foetus improves, and will likely increase as our ability to visually monitor the unborn foetus increases.

[20] It is problematic to link the post-natal and pre-natal stages in this case, as there was a considerable degree of neglect and isolation suffered by the twins during infancy which

Though qualitative studies such as Piontelli's are often held in less scientific regard than are the more quantitative methods discussed previously, the results obtained appear to support the documented conclusions of the quantitative studies. That is to say that the results so far appear to support the contention that late term foetuses and the infants they become are psychologically connected. In Piontelli's words, "while it seems unlikely that children "remember" their experiences within the womb and their birth, such experiences are clearly reflected in their behaviour as they grow and develop".[21]

If Piontelli is correct in her claim that children are unlikely to remember their pre-birth experiences, how can the direct psychological connections required by a strong version of Relation R exist between late term foetuses and the children they become? It would seem that they cannot. While it seems clear that the post-24-week-old foetus and infant do share direct psychological connections in a variety of different forms (sufficient it would seem for there to be both psychological connectedness and continuity between them) the same is not true of the foetus and child, and hence person that it becomes.

Even if it is accepted that there is no direct psychological connection between the post-24-week-old foetus and later person though, it is still possible that there is psychological continuity between the post-24-week-old foetus and person that it becomes. For, as Belzer pointed out:

> Continuity between X and Y requires only a "chain" of strong connectedness between them, and there may be a chain of strong connectedness between X and Y even though there is not even one direct connection between X and Y. For instance, X may be strongly connected to Z_1, Z_1 to Z_2, and Z_n to Y, so we have a chain of strong connectedness (X, Z_1, Z_2, Z_3, Z_n, Y) where there is pairwise strong connectedness between adjacent members of the chain but no direct connections between X and Y. In that case there is continuity between X and Y even though there are no direct psychological connections at all between X and Y.[22]

---

could conceivably have altered any pre-existing psychological or behavioural patterns. (It is interesting to note however, that as a result of their isolation these children suffered from both behavioural and speech retardation, which was only overcome once they were placed in a more "normal" social setting as pre-schoolers.)

[21] Piontelli, *op.cit.* p. 237.
[22] See Belzer, *op.cit.* p. 57.

56 *Interests in Abortion*

With this in mind, if we take X to denote the post-24-week-old foetus, Z_1 the infant, Z_2 the young child, and so on to Y the adult person, it is clear that even though there is a lack of direct psychological connectedness between the foetus and person that it becomes, there is nevertheless psychological continuity as a result of the overlapping chain of direct psychological connections between each of the stages of development.[23] Why, then does a strong version of Relation R not hold between them? The answer I believe may lie in the phenomenon of *infantile amnesia*.

Infantile amnesia is a recognised psychological trait present in all humans, whereby it is apparently not possible to remember anything prior to one's third birthday: any perceived memories prior to this age are said to be reconstructions of someone else's experiences as one's own.[24] Several explanations for *infantile amnesia* have been put forward, the most plausible, however, are those that take account of the cognitive abilities of the pre-three-year-old child.

Memories, as Goswami pointed out, are not "…verbatim recall of past events, but are actually reconstructions of the past based on prior knowledge and personal interpretation. [As such, it is] not possible to isolate memory from other cognitive structures".[25] A one or two year old child for instance, clearly does manifest some complex cognitive skills that are dependent on a functioning memory. Thus, the known existence of various cognitive abilities prior to three years of age is itself evidence of memory prior to three years of age. And, explanations for our inability to access memories laid down during this period need to explain why it is that the reconstructive memory process has no access to the knowledge or experience of this period. To put this another way, it is known that learning, reasoning, and problem solving are all functioning effectively during the period of *infantile amnesia*; it is also known that these cognitive processes rely on a functioning memory. Consequently, it cannot be the case that there is no memory prior to three years of age. This fact needs to

---

[23] There is an assumption here that it is accepted that there are direct psychological connections between each of these stages. The relationship between the foetus and infant is the subject of much of this paper; but so far as the relations between each of the subsequent stages is concerned, there seems to be no controversy attached to the claim that there are clear and direct psychological connections present. Consequently, the issue will not be addressed here.
[24] See Goswami, *op.cit.* for a more detailed discussion of this phenomenon.
[25] *Ibid.* p. 161.

be reconciled with the apparent lack of memory of this period that appears at later stages of development.

One possibility is, as Fivush and Hammond postulated, that *"infantile amnesia* is the absence of abstract knowledge structures for describing the temporal and causal sequences of events".[26] Another plausible explanation is that:

> ...early memories are coded in terms of physical action or pure sensation. [And,] early memories are thus irretrievable...because they are in a different format to later memories which depend on linguistic based encoding and storage.[27]

If either of these theories are correct, a lack of recall of this period in later life does not provide reason to conclude that the pre-3 year old has no functioning memory structures. Clearly they do. The existence of a distinct non-temporal knowledge base, or encoding and storage process based purely on sensory experience merely leads to the conclusion that those memory structures that are functioning prior to three years of age are incompatible with those that function after three years of age. Similarly, the fact that it is not possible in later life to recall infantile or foetal experiences is not sufficient reason to conclude that there can be no psychological connections formed during this period between the foetus and infant and later child.

What it does seem necessary to conclude, is that in the chain of psychological connectedness, of which the psychological continuity between foetus and person is comprised, there is a period composed of "weak links". There is no point at which the overlapping chain of connectedness is actually broken – the foetus is, as we have seen, connected to the infant, the infant to the young child, the young child to the older child, and so on – but between the pre-three year old and post-three year old periods the cognitive processes are transformed. At this time, to continue the analogy, the "chain is created out of different materials: events that were encoded on a purely sensory and action oriented basis,

---

[26] See R. Fivush and N.R. Hammond (1990) 'Autobiographical memory across the pre-school years: Toward reconceptualising childhood amnesia', pp. 223-248 of R. Fivush and J. Hudson (eds) *Knowing and remembering in young children*, Cambridge University Press, New York.

[27] This possibility, put forward by M.L. Howe and M.L. Courage (1993) in 'On resolving the enigma of infantile autism', pp. 305-326, of *Psychological Bulletin*, 113, is also discussed by Goswami, *ibid.*, p. 163.

58 *Interests in Abortion*

come, at three years of age, to be encoded on an abstract linguistic basis".[28] As the chain is not broken by this transformation the existence of Relation R is not negated, it does however lessen the strength of the relation.

Consequently, rather than seeing the presence of a strong R relation as confirmation of one enduring person over time, one must find a term to describe an identity relation weaker than that of actual personhood that is signified by the presence of a weak R relation. The most plausible possibility that is not dependent on the continuation of anything more than a conscious being is that a weak R relation signifies a continuation of a subject of experiences. In which case, the existence of a weak R relation between the foetus and person it becomes would mean that even though the unborn foetus is not an actual person, it is, at least after 24 weeks of development, the very same enduring subject of experience as the person it becomes.

Could the same be said of the pre-24-week-old foetus and embryo though? No. These beings are, as Buckle pointed out, physically continuous with the person they will become, but they cannot be psychologically continuous with any person, for they are not yet conscious subjects of experience. And, as it is, according to the views on identity expressed here, Relation R that is central to the determination of whether two beings are the very same being, and as the R relation is a consequence of psychological connectedness and/or continuity, it follows that prior to the onset of consciousness the human foetus does not share a morally significant identity relation with the person it develops into. In which case, the argument from potential, which rests on the claim that the potential person and the actual person are the very same psychologically enduring being, is applicable only in the case of the post-24-week-old foetus.

Such a conclusion, whilst at odds with the argument from potential as it is commonly expressed, is consistent with the views that were discussed in the previous chapters. We know that a human foetus is not a subject of conscious experience until after the 24th week of its development, and we know that for the presence of Relation R: psychological connectedness and/or continuity, to be even logically possible, the human foetus must first be a subject of experience. Thus, it follows that it is only after the 24th

---

[28] The periods discussed are not intended to be exact, the transformation in a young child's thought processes is a gradual process, and as such the transformation of the psychological relationship being discussed is also gradual. But, in general terms the process would be complete by around three years of age.

week of development that the human foetus can be the very same subject of experiences as the person it will one day become. In which case, according to Parfit's views on identity, we can apply an argument from potential only to the post-24-week-old foetus.

The Potentiality Principle and the Human Foetus

So far we have seen that in order to have an active potential to become a person a human foetus must manifest all of the morally relevant positive causal factors for personhood. On investigation we found that the morally relevant positive causal factors for personhood are an appropriate genetic structure, sentience, consciousness, and a capacity to interact with the social world. We further found that a human foetus first manifests all of these factors at around 24 weeks after conception. We then went on to investigate the issue of identity in more detail. We began with the knowledge that the force of the argument from potential lies in the identity relations between the potential and actual person. For this reason we went on to determine just what identity relation holds between a post-24-week-old foetus and the person it becomes. We found that the post-24-week-old foetus and the person it becomes share a weak version of Relation R such that they are the very same enduring subject of experience.

Having seen that a post-24-week-old foetus with an active potential to become a person is the very same subject of experience as the person it becomes, the next question to ask is what moral significance does the presence of this relation have? In order to answer this question, we will begin with Tooley's two versions of the potentiality principle. The first version that Tooley sets out is dependent on one's definition of personhood encompassing a requirement of biological unity, and is summarily rejected by Tooley on the basis that there is at least a logical possibility that non-biological persons could exist.[29] With this I agree. What I disagree with however, is his revised formulation of the potentiality principle. The revised version states that:

> The destruction of a potential person is intrinsically wrong, and seriously so, where X is a potential person if and only if X is an entity, or system of entities,

---

[29] Tooley, *op.cit.* p. 178.

that has all, or almost all of the properties of a positive sort that together would be causally sufficient to bring it about that X gives rise to a person, and where there are no factors present within X that would block the causal process in question.[30]

On first glance this may appear to be an adequate formulation of the potentiality principle, capturing both the need for an entity to possess an active potential to become a person, and the possibility that non-biological persons could exist. It fails though, I believe, for the reason set forth by Pahel.

Pahel points out that in allowing for the possibility that a potential person is a "system of entities", rather than a unified entity, Tooley fails to clearly distinguish between possible persons and potential persons.[31] This possibility can be avoided by refining Tooley's "Unrestricted Principle" in such a way as to exclude the possibility of "non-unified entities" being considered as potential persons. Moreover, such a restriction is necessary I believe if we are to conceptually distinguish between possible and potential people. One possible way to refine Tooley's principle is simply to remove the clause pertaining to "systems of entities". The principle would then read:

> The destruction of a potential person is intrinsically wrong, and seriously so, where X is a potential person if and only if X is an entity that has all, or almost all of the properties of a positive sort that together would be causally sufficient to bring it about that X gives rise to a person, and where there are no factors present within X that would block the causal process in question.

This formulation not only avoids the conceptual confusion between potential and possible persons, it also avoids the focus of the potentiality principle being placed on potential *per se* rather than on the being that has the potential.[32] This refined version of the potentiality principle is that which I shall take to be the central core of the argument from potential from this point on.

---

[30] *Ibid.* p. 179.
[31] Kenneth R. Pahel (1987) 'Michael Tooley on Abortion and Potentiality', pp. 89-107 of *The Southern Journal of Philosophy*, v.XXV, no.1, p. 97.
[32] See Pahel *ibid.*, for further discussion of this point.

As we saw above, the potentiality principle is, according to both Tooley's and Parfit's understanding of identity, applicable to the post-24-week-old foetus with an active potential to become a person, because the post-24-week-old foetus is the very same enduring psychological entity as the person it will become. And, according to the potentiality principle set out by Tooley and revised here, it is "intrinsically wrong and seriously so" to destroy any being that is a potential person. We have also seen, however, that this principle cannot be used to justify the protection of a pre-24-week-old foetus. This is clearly not a claim that the majority of proponents of an argument from potential are likely to endorse. It is, however, a claim that follows from the argument from potential as it is generally maintained.

For instance, if we look to Buckle's statement of the argument from potential rather than Tooley's, it states that:

> Respect is due to an existing being because it possesses the capacity or power to develop into a being which is worthy of respect in its own right; and respect is due to such a being because it is *the very same being* as the later being into which it develops. The already existing being [the human foetus] has the potential to become a being worthy of respect in its own right.[33]

The majority of proponents of the argument from potential take this claim to apply across the human embryo's and foetus's total developmental period, claiming that the power to develop into a person is a power that is inherent in the human embryo from the very earliest stages of development. On one level, this is clearly true – there is an unbroken physiological continuation between the human embryo and the person it develops into. Physical identity, however, has no inherent moral significance, and in employing an argument from potential there is an implicit claim made that there is a morally significant identity relation between the potential and actual person. In Buckle's words, "Assumptions about identity are intimately connected with the employment of the notion of potentiality".[34] Whether one employs the notion of identity put forward by Parfit (which is the understanding of identity Buckle employs), or that put forward by Tooley, this is undoubtedly the case. It is also the case, as we have seen in this chapter, that only a post-24-week-old foetus can retain

---

[33] Buckle, *op.cit.* p. 93.
[34] *Ibid.* p. 95.

more than a numerical form of identity throughout its development into a person: only a post-24-week-old foetus shares a form of Relation R with the person it becomes.

Consequently, it cannot be the case that an embryo and a pre-24-week-old foetus are the *very same being* (on anything more than a numerical level) as the persons they develop into.[35] Even though the human embryo may manifest the first of the positive causal factors required for the development of personhood – a genetic structure appropriate to the development of personhood, it does not yet manifest any of the other necessary causal factors. And, it is only once all of the morally significant causal factors of personhood become manifest that the argument from potential applies: only at this time can the human foetus be the very same enduring subject of experience as the person it becomes. Only then is respect

> ...due to a being because it possesses the capacity or power to develop into a being which is worthy of respect in its own right: [only then is respect] ...due to such a being because it is the very same being as the later being into which it develops.[36]

At such time as a foetus becomes conscious, it gains a manifest capacity to interact with and learn from the social world (which is evidenced by a vast and growing body of empirical findings). At which time it ceases to be merely a biological object: it becomes from this moment on, a conscious subject of experiences. What is more, it shares at least a weak version of Relation R with the person it becomes and is therefore, from this moment on, the very same subject of experience as the person it will become. Consequently, after the 24th week of a human foetus's development it is intrinsically wrong and seriously so to destroy it.

---

[35] It is worth noting that given Parfit's understanding of identity, numerical identity does not appear to be even a necessary condition for the continuation of an individual.
[36] Buckle, *op.cit.* p. 95.

6 Potential Persons and Interests

The Right to Continued Existence

Even if Tooley were to accept that the post-24-week-old human foetus had an active potential to become a person, and that it is identical to the person it becomes as has been shown in the previous chapters, he would deny that it could have an interest in continued existence. From Tooley's perspective it is only those beings that fall within the scope of his "particular interest principle" that can have an interest in, and hence a right to, continued existence – and clearly potential persons are not such beings. This chapter will examine the rationale behind Tooley's position, and investigate the possibility of broadening it in order for it to encompass potential persons.

It is Tooley's claim that what justifies a being's right to continued existence is its past or presently exercised psychological states. If he were correct in this, then the potential to experience such states in the future would be irrelevant to the determination of a being's moral status. Tooley justifies this position with his "particular interests principle", which says that, "It is a conceptual truth that an entity cannot have a particular right R unless it is at least capable of having some interest I which is furthered by its having right R".[1] In other words, rights only make sense if they promote a specific interest of the being in question.

For instance, it makes no sense, as Tooley points out, to grant a kitten a right to a university education as it clearly has no interest that can be furthered by that right; whereas, it does make sense to grant a kitten a right not to be caused pain, because the kitten's psychological states are such that if it was to be caused pain it is plausible to suppose that it would desire for the pain to cease. Hence, a kitten could have an interest in not experiencing pain, and this interest could be furthered by the kitten having a right not to be caused pain.

---

[1] Tooley, *op.cit*, p. 99.

Tooley derives this principle from Feinberg's more general claim that "...the sorts of beings who can have rights are precisely those who have (or can have) interests".[2] Whilst this general principle is, I think, correct, Tooley's more specific one is not. If the particular interests principle were correct then Tooley's claim that a foetus, as merely a potential person, cannot have a right to continue to exist would also be correct. For, by definition, a potential person is not yet a being with the psychological capacity to desire continued existence. In which case a potential person could not be the sort of being that has an interest in, and therefore a right to, continued existence. There is a problem with Tooley's analysis, however, that once seen makes it plausible to suppose that his limitation of a right to continued existence to self-aware beings only is unjustified.

Objective and Subjective Interests

As Pahel points out, Tooley utilises two different definitions of the term "interests" in order to arrive at the above conclusion, and it is only when these two meanings are left unstated that his argument remains apparently sound.[3] In deriving his particular interests principle Tooley goes through a lengthy process of examining possible counter examples to his position. Firstly, he asks, if one must actually possess a desire in order to have an interest in something, what could one say of an infant that was castrated in order to satisfy the desires of a puritanical religious sect as it matured? Suppose, Tooley says, that the operation is a painless one, and that the infant voices no objection, "...one is [nevertheless] surely tempted to say that individual's rights are being violated".[4] Infants, however, have no desires, interests, or sense of continuing self over time with which to justify such a right according to Tooley's particular interests principle. So how is it possible for the infant's rights to be violated? According to Tooley, "the actions in question, though they do not violate a desire that the individual has at the time of the action, are *contrary to that individual's*

---

[2] J. Feinberg (1974) 'The Rights of Animals and Unborn Generations', pp. 43-68 of William T. Blackstone (ed.), *Philosophy and Environmental Crisis*, cited in Tooley, *ibid.* p. 99.
[3] See Pahel, *op.cit.*
[4] Tooley cited in Pahel *ibid.* p. 92.

interest".⁵ And, the reason why they are contrary to the infant's interests is because the infant could grow up to desire that it had not been castrated. Such an analysis certainly appears plausible, despite the fact that the desire on which the interest is founded is a future desire: a desire that is not a part of the infant's past or presently exercised psychological states.

Furthermore, Tooley continues, what if a situation arose in which a person never came to desire that a certain act had not been done to them? Does this mean that they could not possess a right for that act not to have been carried out at all? Suppose, Tooley says:

> ...one conditions an individual so that she will be satisfied with being a dependent help-mate, and will never have any interest in, for example, intellectually challenging activities to which humans not thus conditioned are naturally attracted.⁶

Even though she may live her whole life and never question her position, surely, Tooley suggests, her rights have in some way been violated. Once again he appears to accept that this is so.

It seems clear from these examples that Tooley recognises the possibility that some rights are objectively ascribable: they are not based on the desires a being has in the present, or has had in the past, but on a desire that an observer can reasonably suppose that being will come to have in the future if it is not prevented from doing so. Thus, it would seem that interests are not just something that can be subjectively experienced, there is also an objective form of interests: interests that an observer can ascribe to a being on the basis of what sort of being it intrinsically is, rather than what properties it has manifested at the time that an act is carried out.

But, in acknowledging the existence of objectively ascribable interests in the case of beings that are unable to desire that thing for themselves, Tooley apparently leaves himself open to the question of why the interest in continued existence is not objectively ascribable. For, as Pahel points out:

> ...the relevant conceptual tie with interests and desires [that Tooley has shown up to this point] would [appear to] be that these are beings that will, unless

---

⁵ Tooley, *op.cit.* p. 112 emphasis added.
⁶ *Ibid.*

prevented, develop the particular interests, desires, and supporting concepts protected by this right in a normal healthy process of maturation.[7]

If this is so, how does Tooley come to the conclusion that as a foetus does not, and has not in the past exhibited the relevant psychological state (that of a concept of itself as a continuing subject of experiences over time), it cannot possess a right to continued existence? Why cannot such an interest be ascribed to beings with an active potential to become persons on the basis that they will come to hold such a concept of themselves if they continue to develop into persons? He apparently does so, as Pahel says, by changing his concept of "interest" from one that is objectively ascribable, to one that is subjectively present.[8] Whereas in the above examples the rights Tooley grants to the infant and the woman are derived from their objectively ascribable interest in not being so treated, the right to continue to exist, he claims, is a special case. Only those beings that subjectively experience their past or present and therefore possess the correlative interest, or those that can be shown to be appropriately psychologically connected to such a being can possess it.

We shall address each of these possibilities in turn. The first of the conditions postulated by Tooley could only be satisfied by actual persons. Thus, if this were a necessary condition it would ensure that potential persons could not possess a right to continue to exist. The apparent rationale behind this condition is that all the rights that he has objectively ascribed to others only exist retrospectively. That is to say that an infant's right not to be castrated only exists if it continues to develop into an adult that could plausibly be supposed to have a desire that it was not castrated, and a woman's right not to be mentally limited via indoctrination only exists if she continues to live after the indoctrination and it can plausibly be supposed that she would desire that she had not been so treated were she aware that she had been. Following this logic, a right to continue to exist would only be granted to those beings that continue to develop into beings that could plausibly be supposed to have a desire to continue to exist. If, however, a being were killed before it could experience such a desire, then there would be no grounds on which to grant it such an interest, and hence no intrinsic wrong would be associated with its death.

---

[7] Pahel, *op.cit.* p. 93.
[8] *Ibid.* p. 95.

This position appears to be problematic, for it does not clearly explain why women or slaves ought to have a right not to be indoctrinated so as to be happy in their subservient positions. If one were absolutely certain that the indoctrination program were successful, there would seem to be no plausible reason to suppose that these people would ever desire that their situation be anything other than what it is. In which case, according to the above exposition, there would be no grounds on which to grant them a right not to be so indoctrinated.

The only way around this problem appears to be by appealing to the type of beings the women and slaves are, and the capacities and outlook they could be presumed to develop were they not interfered with. Such an appeal however, would defeat Tooley's argument, for if a woman can have an interest in not being psychologically prevented from pursuing intellectually challenging pastimes that is derived solely from her natural propensity to do so; then surely a foetus can have an interest in continuing to exist that is derived from its natural propensity to develop into a being with an interest in doing so.

Perhaps it is in order to avoid such a conclusion that Tooley takes "interests" to mean only those interests which are subjectively experienced, either in the past or present, by the being in question. In which case, as Pahel points out, Tooley's claims become true by definition. That is to say that Tooley's case against foetuses having an interest in continued existence rests on his claim that prior to a foetus developing into a subject of consciousness, "it cannot...have any interests at all, and *a fortiori*, it cannot have any interest in its own continued existence".[9] Of course, this is quite correct according to a subjective definition of interests. But then, as was pointed out above, if a subjective definition of interests is employed no infant could have an interest in not being castrated, and no "successfully" programmed woman or slave could have an interest in not having their autonomy and freedom of thought removed. In which case neither the infant nor the woman in the above cases would have had any rights infringed if they were so treated. Such a conclusion is, however, contrary to Tooley's original claims. Thus, it would seem that it is only in the utilisation of both definitions that Tooley has an apparently sound argument. If the alteration in definition of "interests" were to be removed, and the understanding of "interests" remained constant, it would appear

---

[9] Tooley cited in Pahel, *ibid*. p. 96.

that a current right to continue to exist could be ascribed to a potential person on the basis that it will come to have the relevant interest in its future.

Thus, the first of Tooley's conditions for the ascription of a right to continued existence cannot successfully be employed in order to limit a right to continued existence to actual persons, unless one simultaneously accepts a lack of other seemingly fundamental rights such as those of the woman and the infant in the above examples. What then of Tooley's second condition? According to the second possibility Tooley apparently accepts that a right to continued existence would be ascribable, not just to actual persons, but also, in some cases, to those beings that will if not interfered with develop into persons. More specifically the second of Tooley's conditions seemingly allows for a being that has both an active potential to become a person, and that shares an R relation with the person it becomes to possess a right to continued existence.

While this condition clearly seems to encompass the post-24-week-old foetus with the capacities discussed earlier, Tooley did not intend for it to do so. From within Tooley's perspective a post-24-week-old foetus cannot possess an active potential to become a person, because it cannot possess all of the positive causal factors required for the development of personhood. Consequently, Tooley would probably say, a post-24-week-old foetus cannot hold the appropriate psychological relation with the person it develops into. Hence, it cannot be the very same being as that person in anything other than physical form, and cannot have a right to continue to exist based on it potential personhood.

As we have seen in Chapter Two though, if the background causal field within which the positive causal factors of personhood are determined is defined so as to include all morally irrelevant external factors, the post-24-week-old human foetus can possess all of the morally significant causal factors required to possess an active potential to become a person. And, as we have seen, in possessing all of the morally significant positive causal factors of personhood, the post-24-week-old foetus shares a weak version of Relation R with the person it becomes. And, as Tooley has said "…given psychological connectedness [with an actual person], it may be in the interest of such a being to continue to exist even if it does not have, and never did have, a desire for continued existence".[10]

---

[10] *c.f.* unpublished communication with Tooley (1999).

Before it can be accepted that the post-24-week-old foetus, as a being with an active potential to become a person, does have an interest in continued existence, however, Tooley's counter-examples to such a proposition need to be examined.

Brain Damaged People and Frankenstein

Tooley sets forth two cases designed to illustrate why a potential person cannot logically be said to have an interest in continued existence. The first of these concerns a brain-damaged person. Consider, he says, "an adult human being that has suffered brain damage that makes it impossible for the organism to enjoy any consciousness at all, let alone rational self-awareness".[11] This case will not be considered here, other than to say that so long as Tooley's definition of actual personhood is accepted (as it is in this paper), this case poses no problems for the supporter of an argument from potential.

Tooley follows this example with a second scenario, which is directly concerned with potential personhood, but which, as will be seen, is also unproblematic given the understanding of potential personhood developed here. The example involves the creation of a frozen Frankenstein that possesses the capacity for consciousness, but that will not express that capacity until it is unfrozen. Suppose, Tooley says, that this being was programmed with the beliefs, attitudes, capacities and personality traits of Billy Graham, but that just prior to thawing the being out, the creators changed their mind and reprogrammed it with the beliefs, attitudes, capacities and personality traits of Bertrand Russell.[12] Intuitively there would seem to be no wrong done here, and if as Tooley claims only actual persons can possess an interest in continued existence, that intuition is supported. But, Tooley seems to be arguing, if one believes that an active potential for personhood is sufficient to grant a being an interest in continued existence surely the reprogramming of Frankenstein would be seen to have resulted in the destruction of a potential person, and would consequently be seen as a morally wrong act. I disagree with this conclusion.

---

[11] Tooley, *op.cit.* pp. 152-3.
[12] *Ibid.* p .154.

By definition, a potential person does not possess the complex psychological capacities being altered by Frankenstein's creators. Once Frankenstein was conscious and had manifested these complex psychological attributes he would likely be an actual person; and prior to consciousness he can have no psychological traits at all. In which case, whether the programming of Frankenstein will reflect Billy Graham's or Bertrand Russel's psychology once he is thawed out is irrelevant. And, furthermore, given the understanding of potential personhood that is being developed in this paper, it seems more plausible to claim that Frankenstein has a latent potential to become a person rather than an active potential, as it has within it a factor which will prevent the manifestation of personhood: namely, it is frozen. In which case, it could, without challenging any of the arguments put forward in this paper, be accepted that Tooley is correct in his analysis of the situation.

The Post-24-Week-Old Foetus's Right to Continued Existence

As can be seen, neither of Tooley's examples wholly supports the conclusion he intends them to. In the first case, an argument in favour of objectively ascribing an interest in continued existence to a being with an active potential to become a person is unaffected. Whilst in the latter case the understanding of potential personhood put forward in this paper makes it clear that changing a potential person's as yet unexperienced complex thought processes cannot mean we are destroying that being, for by definition a potential person cannot be the "owner" of any such thought processes. Thus, Tooley has, I think, failed to put forward a convincing case against the ascription of a right to continued existence to potential persons. Despite his examples to the contrary, it still appears to be plausible to maintain that such is the case. Furthermore, in broadening his stance in order to encompass cases such as the indoctrinated woman discussed above, Tooley leaves open the possibility that rights can be attributed to beings on the basis of what those beings can plausibly be supposed to become in the normal course of their development.

Consequently, whilst Tooley's "psychological states" view of personhood can be justified by Feinberg's general claim relating interests to rights, his limitation of the consequences of that view to actual persons is unsuccessful. Tooley has not given sufficient reason to refute the possibility of an objectively ascribable right to continued existence: neither his case for differentiating this right from other rights, nor his case against potential persons having a right to continued existence has strongly supported his position. And, what is more, Tooley's acknowledgment of the possibility that the presence of Relation R may grant a being a right to continue to exist, makes it plausible to suppose that the human foetus from 24 weeks of development onwards can, given that it shares Relation R with the person it becomes, have an interest in continued existence on the basis of its active potential to become a person. Thus, given that the post-24-week-old foetus has such an interest, it can be concluded that the post-24-week-old human foetus therefore has a right to continued existence, and that killing it is therefore *prima facie* a wrong act.

7 Moral Asymmetry

The Principle of Moral Symmetry

Having found that human foetuses from 24 weeks of development onwards can plausibly be held to possess a right to continued existence, and that it is therefore *prima facie* wrong to destroy them does not, however, provide a total response to Tooley's claims. According to Tooley it is inconsistent to assert that it is intrinsically wrong to destroy a potential person, unless one simultaneously asserts that it is intrinsically wrong to fail to actualise a possible person. If correct, this claim would highlight a serious problem for every argument from potential, for it would mean that if one were to argue that abortion is morally problematic, one would also have to support the claim that contraception is morally problematic. How then should one respond to this claim?

To arrive at his somewhat startling conclusion Tooley argues that, all things being equal, there is no morally significant difference between killing and failing to save. He then goes on to apply the principle he derives from this claim (the Principle of Moral Symmetry) to a pair of cases, one of which is a potential person, the other of which is a merely possible person. I will argue here, that while the Principle of Moral Symmetry is acceptable, Tooley's application of it to a pair of cases consisting of two different types of beings invalidates his overall argument.

The principle of moral symmetry, as Tooley states it, says: "Let C be any type of causal process where there is some type of occurrence E, such that processes of type C would possess no intrinsic moral significance were it not for the fact that they result in occurrences of type E".[1] It follows from this basic principle, Tooley says, that:

> The characteristic of being an act of intervening in a process of type C that prevents the occurrence of an outcome of type E makes an action intrinsically wrong to precisely the same degree as does the characteristic of being an act of

---

[1] Tooley, *op cit.* p. 186.

insuring that a causal process of type C, which it was in one's power to initiate, does not get initiated.[2]

Put simply, this principle entails that "being a case of killing, and being a case of failing to save, are equally weighty wrong-making characteristics".[3] For, although cases of killing and failing to save often appear to lead to different moral intuitions concerning their degree of wrongness, if one holds the morally relevant factors constant across both cases, these apparent differences disappear.

This becomes clear if one builds into the examples statements concerning the identicality of morally relevant factors such as the motivation behind the action/inaction, the expenditure of energy required for both, and the consequences of both, killing and failing to save appear to be morally equal. For example, when Tooley discusses the case of Jones shooting Smith and compares this to Jones letting Smith be killed by a bomb that he could easily have warned him of, there appears to be no morally significant difference between Jones' acting and failing to act. In both cases, Jones wants Smith dead, and Smith dies as a result of Jones acting/not acting on his desire. Thus, in the examples Tooley puts forth in support of the principle of Moral Symmetry it would seem that his conclusion that there is no morally significant difference between acting and failing to act is correct. The Principle of Moral Symmetry does appear to be a valid principle. Tooley's further claim that "when people feel that the principle is unacceptable it is because they are considering pairs of cases that differ in other morally significant respects",[4] however, explains why it is that the Principle fails in the case of potential and possible people.

In his failing to consider this possibility when arguing that killing a potential person is morally equivalent to failing to actualise a possible person, it is evident that Tooley believes that a pair of cases in which one party is a merely possible person and the other is a potential person does not differ in any morally significant respect to the cases he presents as support for the principle. This, I believe, is an implausible position.

What is noticeable in all of the cases Tooley presents as support for the Principle of Moral Symmetry is that the affected parties are all morally equivalent actual persons. In the above-mentioned scenario, for instance,

---

[2] *Ibid.*
[3] *Ibid.* p. 187
[4] Tooley, *op.cit.*

the person killed and the person not saved are the very same person. In the case in question here however, neither of the parties is an actual person. And, what is more, there is no reason to suppose that a potential person and a possible person are morally equivalent beings. In other words, Tooley provides support for the Moral Symmetry Principle in cases involving killing an actual person and failing to save an actual person; and from these cases, when all other differences are held equal, one can conclude that the principle is a valid one. But, to move from a pair of cases involving the killing of an actual person and the failure to save an actual person, to a pair of cases involving the killing of an actual person and the failure to save a non-person would not be justified by this conclusion. Not because the principle is in itself wrong, but because there is no evidence provided by the prior argument to suggest that the two beings are morally equivalent.

For the same reason Tooley's application of the Principle of Moral Symmetry to potential and possible persons is unjustified, for there is no justification for the assumption that they are a morally symmetrical pair. Rather, the assumption is implicit in Tooley's formulation of the principle itself. Just as was the case in his formulation of the potentiality principle that was discussed in the previous chapter, the Principle of Moral Symmetry as Tooley states it, implicitly removes any moral distinction between potential and possible persons by focusing on causal processes rather than on the beings in question. In doing so, Tooley manages to equate a living foetus and a set of conditions that could result in a living foetus. He does this be placing both under the umbrella term of "causal processes that result in persons". This is a questionable definition of potential persons though, for it avoids the need to recognise that potential persons, unlike possible persons are actually existing beings. Consequently, it obscures the very morally significant difference that makes potential and possible persons an asymmetrical pair.[5]

---

[5] In response to this, it is not sufficient to point out that the distinction is built into the Moral Symmetry Principle itself: that one is comparing interfering with a causal process that exists, with failing to initiate a comparable causal process. For, once a distinction is made between the causal processes in question and the beings those processes affect, the application of the principle to two different types of beings must be further justified.

An Asymmetrical Application of the Principle of Moral Symmetry

What then is the asymmetry? As we have seen in previous chapters a morally relevant potential person is a sentient, and psychologically aware being, it is the possessor of actual experiences, and it will, if it is not prevented from doing so, develop into an actual person. It is not, as Tooley appears to believe, merely a causal process with a morally significant outcome, it is an actually existing being undergoing a causal process, and it already has within itself something of moral significance. A merely possible person, on the other hand, does not yet exist. As such it cannot be the possessor of any psychological or physiological experiences, it cannot be identical to any person that will come to exist in the future, it cannot even have a latent potential to become a person. It is merely a biological object (an unfertilised egg for instance) with a passive potential to become a person. And, as was shown in Chapter Two, no entity or object with a merely passive potential to become a person could be morally considerable on the basis of its potential. Thus, the asymmetry between a potential and a possible person is that in one case there is a conscious subject of experiences undergoing the process of becoming a person while in the other case there is no subject of experiences undergoing any process: at most there is a biological object with a passive potential to produce a being capable of undergoing that process. As Pahel said,

> ...whether or not we actually ascribe ...rights to a foetus, [a foetus is] conceptually cleared as a potential rights holder. However, prior to conception, we do not have a being that is even conceptually a possible holder of rights (even though there may be a "causal process" that has been initiated).[6]

How then, can one say that there is no morally significant difference between a potential person and a possible person, as Tooley believes to be the case? In one case, there is an active potential to become a person, and in the other case there is at most only a passive potential to become a person. To assume moral equivalence of two such beings, and on that basis place them both under the umbrella term of "causal processes" is no more acceptable than it would be to assume that potential and actual persons are morally equivalent beings, and to place them both under the umbrella term

---

[6] Pahel, *op.cit.* p. 102.

of "living organisms" on the basis of that assumption. The resulting application of the Principle of Moral Symmetry to either pair of cases would be invalid, as it would rest on an unsubstantiated definition of the parties involved that obscures the morally relevant differences between them.

Furthermore, we have seen in the preceding pages that the post-24-week-old human foetus with an active potential to become a person, shares a weak version of Relation R with the person it becomes, such that it is the very same enduring subject of experiences as that person. On this basis the post-24-week-old human foetus has an interest in continued existence; whereas a merely possible person can have no such right as it cannot, even conceptually, be the holder of any interests on which to base that right.

These differences are morally significant differences, and consequently the application of the Principle of Moral Symmetry to a pair of cases one of which is a potential person, the other of which is a possible person is invalid. As Tooley said, it is the presence of morally significant differences between the cases in question that leads to an invalid application of the principle. In which case, Tooley's claim that if one accepts that it is wrong to destroy a potential person one is also committed to an acceptance of the wrongness of failing to actualise merely possible persons has no justifiable basis.

Tooley's Kittens

Despite this conclusion it is still useful, I think, to juxtapose Tooley's well known "kitten example" with an equivalent human example in order to highlight the moral asymmetry that exists between potential and possible persons. Suppose, Tooley says, that a serum was developed which when injected into kittens will cause them to develop into persons, with "all the psychological properties associated with adult persons".[7] And suppose, he says, that one of a pair of kittens has been injected with the serum but has not as yet developed the properties of a person, while the other kitten has not been injected at all. In human terms the kitten that has not been injected could be paralleled with an ova that has not been fertilised, while

---

[7] *Ibid.* p. 191

the kitten that has been injected could be compared with a post-24-week-old foetus.[8]

Now let's suppose, Tooley says, that the first kitten is injected with a "neutralising substance" that will prevent the continuation of the kitten's development into a person, and compare this act with intentionally refraining from injecting the serum into the second kitten. "Where is the morally significant difference?" he asks. It is his contention that whilst it is possible that both of these actions are seriously wrong, the moral symmetry principle entails "that the former is no more seriously wrong than the latter".[9] That is to say that destroying a potential person is no more seriously wrong than failing to actualise a possible person. In human terms, however, this pair of cases appears to be somewhat less symmetrical than Tooley believes it to be. In the first case the human parallel is the neutralisation of a post-24-week-old foetus's potential to become a person; in the second case the parallel is intentionally not fertilising the human ova.[10]

The moral distinction between these two cases is not a result of our acting in one case and failing to act in the other. It is based on there being an actually existing potential person that possesses interests that is harmed in one instance, and there being no being with interests that could be harmed in the other instance. Prior to the damage being caused to the foetus it had an active potential to become a person, after the damage the foetus no longer has that capacity though it will continue to develop into a non-self-aware human.

This case could be closely paralleled with the example of a woman being conditioned so that she will be satisfied with being a dependent helpmate, and will never have any interest in, for example, intellectually challenging activities to which humans not thus conditioned are naturally

---

[8] The reason for paralleling the latter scenario with a post-24-week-old foetus, and not merely a human embryo or fertilised ovum is that Tooley says the kitten that has been injected is a potential person, and in human terms, as we have already seen, the pre-24-week-old foetus does not have an active potential to become a person.

[9] *Ibid.*

[10] To say at this stage that one cannot successfully parallel the kittens in the example with human ova because they are radically different entities is to miss the point of the analogy. Tooley explicitly says that "one could replace references to kittens and special chemicals by references to unfertilised human egg cells and spermatozoa, and the argument offered would be unaffected". In which case, the fact that in reality kittens are conscious, aware of their environment, and so on is irrelevant to the issue at hand.

attracted, that Tooley uses in his discussion of what beings can possess interests.[11] Tooley suggests, as was discussed in Chapter Six, that the woman's rights in this example have in some way been violated. Similarly, in this case, the foetus is manipulated in such a way that despite its continued existence, it never possesses the capacities and desires that it would have had had it not been interfered with, and its rights do in some way seem to have been violated. In the case of the ova though, there is no correlative interest in continued existence that could have been violated. At most, there is an object with the passive potential to become a person that has been left unharmed in its original state. Tooley's claims of symmetry are most problematic at this stage, as there appears to be a clear moral distinction between the act and omission in question.

However, having accepted that there is no moral distinction to be made in the previous pair of cases, Tooley goes on to compare the kitten who has had the serum neutralised with a kitten that has never been injected. "It seems no more seriously wrong to kill the former than the latter", he says.[12] With this claim I agree, for the harm to the potential person has already been done. There is no longer any being with an interest in continued existence; the foetus that is aborted at this stage of the argument no longer has the capacity to become a person. And, as it is no longer possible for it to develop into a person, no intrinsic wrongness could arise through the violation of an interest in continued existence were it to be killed.

If this is so, Tooley continues, how about comparing the killing of a kitten that has been injected with the serum but which has not yet had it neutralised, with the killing of a kitten that has never been injected? Tooley claims that it follows from the previous two steps that it is no more wrong to neutralise the serum in the kitten that is a potential person and then kill it, than it is to kill the kitten that has never been a potential person. Furthermore, he says, one way to neutralise the serum is simply to kill the kitten, and from the previous argument it follows that it is no more wrong to do so than it is to kill the kitten who has not been injected. Thus, Tooley goes on to conclude, killing the kitten that is a potential person can be no more seriously wrong than failing to inject the kitten that never was a person.

---

[11] Tooley, *op.cit*. p. 112.
[12] *Ibid*.

Such an argument clearly only follows if one accepts Tooley's previous claims. If one disagrees with his earlier conclusions there remains no reason to accept his final conclusion. In human terms the killing of both of the kittens can be equated with the killing of a healthy post-24-week-old foetus, and the destruction of an unfertilised ovum. In one case an object with no interests is destroyed, and hence no wrong is done; whilst in the other case a being with an interest in continued existence is destroyed, and consequently a direct wrong is done. The distinction in the moral wrongness of the two cases, as I noted in discussion of the first scenario, is not based on our acting in one case and our failing to act in the other. It is based on the type of beings in question, one of which, as we have see in earlier chapters, has an interest in continued existence, the other of which has no such interest. It is clear that there is no moral symmetry between the two cases.

As Tooley correctly points out the Principle of Moral Symmetry was carefully formulated to ensure its applicability to pairs of cases in which one being is a potential person and the other a possible person. However, it becomes clear on examination of the above argument that in his labelling of potential people and possible people as morally indistinct "causal processes" Tooley has, perhaps unintentionally, hidden the morally significant differences between them. Once potential persons and possible persons are differentiated from each other in terms of the interests they possess, the apparent symmetry between the two is lost.[13] The Principle of Moral Symmetry applies, as Tooley says, only in cases in which all morally significant differences are removed. Consequently, in applying it to a pair of cases involving different types of beings – beings with differing potentials, capacities, and interests – Tooley infringes this requirement.

One cannot show that there is no morally significant difference between destroying one being and failing to actualise another when there are morally significant differences between those two beings. Consequently, Tooley's claim that in order to coherently maintain that it is morally wrong to destroy a potential person one must also assent to the claim that it is morally wrong to fail to actualise a possible person does not follow from

---

[13] It should be noted that the arguments I have put forward here apply only to beings with an active potential to become a person, the same cannot be said of being with a latent potential to become persons.

the Principle of Moral Symmetry. Cases involving potential persons and possible persons are different types of cases; there are morally significant differences between them which invalidate any conclusions drawn on the basis of the Principle of Moral Symmetry. Thus, one can coherently assert that the killing of a human foetus with an active potential to become a person is morally wrong, while simultaneously asserting that contraception is not morally wrong.

8 The Practical Consequences

The Case So Far

Having seen that there is no inconsistency in asserting that it is wrong to destroy a potential person whilst denying that it is wrong to fail to actualise a possible person, we should now look to the practical consequences of such an assertion. In general it follows from this position that one can claim that contraception is not morally problematic, but that abortion, if it involves the death of a foetus with an active potential to become a person is morally wrong. As we have seen though, the human foetus does not have an active potential throughout the totality of its foetal stage. Consequently, the arguments developed in this paper do not justify the claim that abortion is always wrong. What exactly is justified by the arguments presented here? What can we say of the IVF and embryo experimentation debate? What can we say of early and mid term abortions? What can we conclude in regards to our treatment of non-human animals? And, how should conflicts between a mother's and a foetus's rights and interests be resolved? These questions form the basis of this chapter. But, before addressing these issues, a short review of the case put forward in the preceding pages will be useful.

We began with Tooley's claim that the human foetus's potential to become a person is not fully active, because human foetuses cannot possess all of the positive causal factors of personhood. We found that the determination of whether each of the factors required for the development of personhood is a part of the background causal field or a one of the significant causal factors is in some ways an arbitrary choice. It was argued, however, that as external factors are generally irrelevant to a being's moral standing, only the internal causal factors required for the development of personhood ought to be classified as morally significant causal factors, and that all of the external factors required for the development of personhood therefore ought to be placed within the background causal field. That is to say that all of the external factors required for the development of personhood ought to be assumed to be present for the sake of determining a being's moral status. Given this definition of the background causal field in the determination of a being's moral status, it was found that despite their physical dependence on others, human foetuses could logically possess all of the positive causal factors necessary to become persons, and that human foetuses could consequently possess an active potential to become persons.

Following this we examined human foetal development in order to discover what positive causal factors contributed to their development into persons, and at what stage in their development human foetuses could be said to possess all of the necessary factors. It was found that in order for a human foetus to develop into a person it had to possess a species-typical genetic structure, it had to be sentient, it had to be conscious of its environment on a psychological level, and it had to possess a manifest capacity to interact with the social world. It was further found: that once a human foetus manifested this final capacity it possessed all of the morally significant positive causal factors necessary for it to become a person.[1] It was concluded, on the basis of all currently available empirical evidence that this capacity becomes manifest at around the 24th week of a human foetus's development. Accordingly, it was concluded that from the 24th week of development onwards, human foetuses had an active potential to become persons.

This position was further strengthened by an examination of Parfit's identity criterion. Parfit's criterion for identity requires "Relation R (psychological continuity and/or connectedness)" to be present. We found that a strong version of relation R is not shared by the human foetus and the person it becomes, but that there is a weak R relation between the post-24-week-old foetus and the person it becomes which is sufficient to show that they are the very same enduring subject of experience. On this basis we concluded that Tooley was incorrect to say that there is no intrinsic wrong associated with the destruction of human foetuses: that, contrary to Tooley's claim, human foetuses are the very same enduring subject of experience as the persons they will become, and that the person's interest

---

[1] Due to the centrality of this issue to the arguments presented in this paper, it is important to emphasise again what is meant by "a capacity to interact with the social world". The type of interaction pointed to by this condition, as was discussed in Chapter Two, is not an unconscious reaction to physical stimuli. Rather, it is a psychological awareness – a capacity to actively interact with actual persons. This is not to say, however, that any being with a capacity to interact with the social world ought to be granted an interest in continued existence. It is only when this capacity is combined with a genetic structure suitable for the development of personhood, that such a right could become an issue.

in continuing to exist which will be expressed in the future grounds the foetus's interest in continuing to exist in the present. To put this another way, it was found that a post-24-week-old foetus that is a subject of momentary experiences resulting in interests, is the very same subject of experience as the person that is a subject of non-momentary interests. And, that because the post-24-week-old foetus and the person it becomes are the very same enduring subject of experiences, the non-momentary interests the foetus will experience at a later stage of its existence are sufficient to ground its interests in continued existence at its present stage. Therefore, it was concluded that as the post-24-week-old foetus has an interest in continuing to exist it would be *prima facie* wrong to kill it.

Finally we addressed Tooley's claim that it is inconsistent to assert that it is wrong to destroy potential persons without simultaneously accepting that it is wrong to fail to actualise possible persons. On examination of this argument, it was found that Tooley had failed to exclude all morally relevant differences between the two cases and that consequently his argument was not sound.

What in practical terms follows from these claims? The complicated nature of this question requires that it be addressed in several stages. Firstly, the issues that are raised in regards to our treatment of human embryos will be addressed. Secondly, issues related to the treatment of the pre-24-week-old foetus that does not yet have an active potential to become a person will be examined. And finally, we will examine issues related to the treatment of the post-24-week-old foetus that does have an active potential to become a person. Where relevant we will also address the possible conflict that could arise between the foetus's and the mother's interests during each of these stages. The interests of non-human animals with capacities parallel to the human embryo and foetus will also be examined

Practicalities and Human Embryos

We have seen that prior to 24 weeks of development a human embryo and foetus (whilst numerically identical to the person it becomes) is not psychologically continuous with that person, nor does it have an active potential to become that person. The only way in which the embryo and the person it develops into can be said to be continuous is on a purely physical level. Numerical/physical continuity is not, however, a morally significant form of identity. There is thus no way in which the human embryo could have an interest in continued existence grounded in its present capacities or in its future desires. In which case no interest could be thwarted were the human embryo to be aborted.

For the same reasons, the human embryo *qua* embryo could not be harmed by IVF practices or embryo experimentation. It has no interests in the present; it is not psychologically connected or continuous with any being that will come to have an interest in the future. Consequently no direct wrong can be done by preventing its continued existence. It should be noted, however, that while no direct wrong can be done to a human embryo via these practices, the side effects either of early abortion or embryo experimentation could make such practices indirectly wrong in some instances. Such side effects could arise in two ways: either as effects on other presently existing people such as the parents of the embryos, or as effects on future persons born as a result of embryo experimentation prior to implantation. In the latter case, even though no direct wrong can be done to a human embryo by destroying it, experimentation which occurred prior to implantation which resulted in harm being caused to the future person born as a result of the experimentation would be indirectly wrong. It is possible, for instance, that an indirect wrong could be done to a future person were a human embryo to be tampered with in such a way as to reduce that future person's quality of life. In this and the former case, however, the harms caused are not intrinsic to the acts themselves; they are indirect harms, and as such arguments for their moral wrongness would rest largely on consequentialist arguments not developed here. As such the possibility will not be explored further other than to note that a lack of intrinsic wrongness should not be taken as grounds for assuming that an act will always be morally acceptable.

Practicalities and Pre-24-Week-Old Human Foetuses

What of the post-embryonic but pre-24-week-old foetus though, are the consequences of the argument developed in these pages the same at this stage of development as they are at the embryonic stage of development? No. There is one very significant difference between the human embryo and the pre-24-week-old foetus: even though it possesses no interest in continued existence, a pre-24-week-old foetus may have an interest in not being caused pain. Along the continuum of development from embryonic to conscious foetal stage there may well be a point at which the human foetus is able to experience pain even though it is not yet consciously aware of its environment. Whether or not this is actually the case is dependent on whether a degree of sensation can be experienced by the foetus prior to the functional development of the cerebral cortex. If indeed a functioning thalamus is the minimal requirement for the sensation of pain, as many theorists believe,[2] then even though the pre-24-week-old foetus has no interest in continuing to exist it would possess an interest in not being caused pain. For, as Singer said, "if a being suffers, there can be no moral justification for refusing to take that suffering into consideration".[3]

To determine the relevance of this point to our treatment of pre-24-week-old foetuses we must ask two questions: (1) what is the basis of the claim that the pre-24-week-old foetus is able to experience pain despite it not having an active cerebral cortex? And, (2) are abortion procedures likely to cause pain if such a claim is true? As we saw in Chapter Three, there is a considerable degree of controversy over a foetus's capacity to experience pain prior to its 24th week. Indeed, whether or not there is some perception of pain in brain centres below the cerebral cortex is still an open question. Clearly, the answer to the question of the pre-24-week-old foetus's capacity to feel pain is an empirical one though, and as such any considerations concerning this capacity ought to be based on the latest scientific information available. And, given that we do not yet have a sufficient degree of scientific knowledge to provide a definitive answer to the question of foetal pain, we may need to rest the guidelines for the treatment of human foetuses on a basis other than simple empirical proof.

Such guidelines should, at the very least, match our standards in relation to the burden of proof that applies to the experimental use of non-human animals. Surprisingly, however, such is not the case. The NH&MRC guidelines for the treatment of experimental animals require that the possibility of sentience be taken into account and anaesthesia provided when dealing with non-human mammalian foetuses.[4] But, unlike the code of practice concerned with the care and treatment of non-human animals,

---

[2] See Chapter Three above, and the *Commission of Inquiry into Foetal Sentience, op.cit.*

[3] P. Singer (1993) *Practical Ethics* (2nd ed.) Cambridge University Press, Cambridge.p. 57.

[4] NH&MRC (1997) Australian Code of Practice for the Care and Use of Animals for Scientific Purposes, September, p. 28.

the NH&MRC statement concerned with out treatment of unborn humans provides no acknowledgment of the possibility of foetal awareness. Rather, the statement discusses the human embryo, foetus and human foetal tissue as if they were the same thing: that is, as "the whole or part of what is called the embryo, foetus or neonate, from the time of implantation to the time of complete gestation".[5] Given such an open categorisation, which as we have seen encompasses a broad spectrum of psychological activity (from no psychological activity at all in the embryonic stage, through to a capacity for both an awareness of and ability to interact with other human persons in the final stages of foetal development), there is bound to be difficulty in determining appropriate standards of treatment. There is however, no acknowledgment of this difficulty in the NH&MRC statement. The closest acknowledgment that there is any possibility of foetal pain is in the statement that "dissection of the foetus should not be carried out while a heart beat is still apparent or there are other obvious signs of life".[6]

This position is clearly contrary to the current scientific information which strongly suggests the possibility of human foetal sentience prior to 24 weeks of development. Even prior to 24 weeks of development it is known that human foetal metabolic stress responses to invasive procedures are three to five times greater than in adults undergoing similar types of surgery.[7] It is also known that a higher concentration of anaesthesia is required to sedate the human foetus; and that premature neonates will withdraw from smaller degrees of pain than do full-term infants or adults.[8] Furthermore, there is widespread agreement that the neurotransmitters that mediate pain are present by the middle of the second trimester of pregnancy, but that the neurotransmitters that inhibit pain are not found

---

[5] See the NH&MRC (1998) *Draft Statement on Ethical Conduct in Research Involving Humans*, July, Supplementary note 5 *The Human Foetus and the Use of Human Foetal Tissue*.
[6] Ibid.
[7] See, for instance, Hepper *op.cit.* and Liley *op.cit.*
[8] See, Xenophon Giannakoulopoulos *et al.* (1994) 'Foetal plasma cortisol and beta-endorphin response to intrauterine needling', *The Lancet*, v.344 (8915), July 9, pp. 77-82. See also, KJS Anna *et al.* (1987) 'Randomised trial of fentanyl anaesthesia in preterm babies undergoing surgery', *The Lancet*, no.8524, pp. 62-66; and K.J.S Anna and P.R. Hickey (1987) 'Pain and its effects in the human neonate and foetus', *The New England Journal of Medicine*, v377, pp. 1321-1329.

before 28 weeks of pregnancy.[9] In other words, it is well established that the pre-24-week-old human foetus reacts strongly, and in a way that is physically comparable to adult humans, when they undergo procedures that would cause pain to adults. The neurotransmitters necessary for pain sensation are present prior to 24 weeks of development, but the neurotransmitters required to diffuse painful sensations are not present. Correspondingly, infants born prematurely, before the chemicals to diffuse pain are present react to smaller degrees of pain and require more anaesthesia to sedate them. Added to these facts are the known behavioural responses of human foetuses in response to touch from 5.5 weeks of development, and the decreased level of complications and convalescence time required of human foetuses and neonates if anaesthesia is administered prior to invasive procedures.[10]

These findings may not provide indisputable proof that the pre-24-week-old foetus does feel pain, but they do give significant support to that assertion. As the *Commission of Inquiry into Foetal Sentience* found:

> ...almost everyone now agrees that unborn babies have the ability to feel pain by 24 weeks after conception and there is a considerable and growing body of evidence that the foetus may be able to experience suffering from around 11 weeks of development.[11]

Given currently accepted standards of treatment in regards to other mammalian foetuses, empirical support for the mere possibility that human foetuses can feel pain ought to be sufficient to alter our treatment of them. The burden of proof should, as is the case with other species, be shifted from those that claim that the human foetus can feel pain to those that believe that it cannot. For, as the NH&MRC statement on non-human species states, "unless there is specific evidence to the contrary investigators must assume foetuses have the same requirements for anaesthesia and analgesia as do adult animals of the species".[12] Such is not the case though. Consequently, it may well be the case that a significant amount of avoidable suffering is caused to pre-24-week-old foetuses, not

---

[9] *Ibid.*
[10] *Ibid.*
[11] *Commission of Inquiry into Human Sentience*, Statement of Main Findings, *op.cit.* (page number unavailable).
[12] NH&MRC (1997) *op.cit.* p. 28.

only during life-saving interuterine surgical treatment, but also during abortion procedures.

With such a significant possibility that the human foetus prior to 24-weeks of development is capable of feeling pain, the lack of recognition by the NH&MRC is inconsistent with the rationale behind their guidelines concerning the treatment of all other mammalian species. Consistency, in scientific and medical practices would seem to demand therefore, that we apply the same standards to the treatment of human foetuses as we do to all other mammalian species. Consequently, the possibility of their feeling pain is a factor that ought to be taken into account whenever they are subjected to invasive procedures. Abortion, as a highly invasive procedure, clearly falls within the parameters of this statement. The pre-24-week-old foetus does not have an interest in continued existence, and hence killing it is not an intrinsically wrong act, but as a being that may well be capable of experiencing pain, the pre-24-week-old human foetus ought to be treated as if it has an interest in not being caused pain.

Currently acceptable abortion practices in Australia make no concession to such an interest however. In the first trimester of pregnancy abortion practices include dilation and curettage (d&c) with dismemberment of the live foetus prior to extraction. This procedure can take up to ten minutes to complete and frequently results in the severance of limbs prior to death.[13] Suction curettage is also practiced at this stage of pregnancy. It takes a similar amount of time to complete as does d&c, and also involves death as a result of dismemberment. Though in this case the severance of limbs is a result of strong suction being applied to the foetus that is still attached to the mother via the umbilical cord. Further into a pregnancy d&c with dismemberment is still an accepted option, as is d&c with intact delivery (also known as partial birth abortion). The insertion of hypertonic saline solution into the uterus is another method used during the middle stages of pregnancy. This method can take up to two hours to kill the foetus and produces severe acid-like burns, that have been likened to those produced by napalm, prior to death. Less often used but also available is an injection of prostaglandin to induce labour, constrict foetal circulation, and cause foetal cardiac arrest.

Of these methods only the latter appears to be likely to result in a relatively swift and painless death. It is not however, a predominantly

---

[13] See Noonan *op.cit.* p. 211.

utilised method in either first or second trimester abortions. Perhaps surprisingly the one other tool of abortion that is capable of killing the foetus quickly and with minimal pain is apparently rarely employed at any stage of pregnancy. It is possible to administer an intracardiac injection of potassium chloride to the foetus, resulting in an almost immediate cessation of the heart beat prior to the abortion procedure continuing, and consequently causes little or no suffering to the foetus. This method is not, however, standard practice, it is seemingly utilised only to minimise the parental and staff distress that could eventuate from a live birth.[14]

As can be seen, current abortion practices make no concession to the possibility of foetal suffering. Yet, if those theorists who claim that a pre-24-week-old foetus can feel pain are correct, then of those foetuses that are aborted a very large percentage suffer immensely before they die. This possibility alone ought to be sufficient to change acceptable abortion practices and bring them into line with our treatment of non-human foetuses. Abortion may not be an intrinsically wrong act prior to 24 weeks post-conception, but the causing of unnecessary pain and suffering to a sentient being is an intrinsically wrong act. Consequently, if there are procedures available to stop the foetal heart swiftly and relatively painlessly, and these procedures do not inflict a disproportionate burden on the woman, then not to adopt these procedures when possible is a wrong act and ought not to be an option.

Practicalities and Post-24-Week-Old Human Foetuses

The case against our current abortion practices becomes considerably stronger when discussing the post-24-week-old foetus. As has been shown in the preceding pages, after 24 weeks post-conception it is no longer merely a possibility that the human foetus can experience pain: the available evidence clearly supports the presence of such a capacity. As a result the post-24-week-old foetus undoubtedly has an interest in not being caused pain. Furthermore, as a being that has an active potential to become a person, and a being that is the very same enduring subject of experience as the person it becomes, the post-24-week-old foetus has an interest in

---

[14] See Victorian Government (1998) *Victorian Government Report on late term terminations of pregnancy*, April, found at http://hna.ffh.vic.gov.au/abs/report.

92 *Interests in Abortion*

continued existence. Killing it is therefore a direct infringement of that interest, and abortion after 24 weeks of development is consequently a *prima facie* wrong.

Once again, however, current abortion practices in Australia and elsewhere do not recognise any foetal interests either in regards to pain or continued life. It is true that in Victoria "it is an indictable offence to destroy the life of a child capable of being born alive".[15] But, despite this legislative boundary post-24-week-old foetuses are aborted − often painfully, and always with the intention of killing them.[16] The two methods used in Victoria at this stage of development, as stated by the *Victorian Government Report into Late Term Abortions* are: (1) induction of labour with prostaglandin, sometimes with a foetal intracardiac injection of potassium chloride, and (2) dilation and extraction with prostaglandin. The first of these methods is a prolonged process, closely following the course of a normal labour and delivery for the mother, and may therefore be the source of considerable distress to the parents. The second method is similar to that commonly employed in earlier stages of pregnancy: that is, it involves either the *in utero* dismemberment of the foetus prior to delivery, or an intact breech delivery followed by the destruction of the foetus's brain via a hole drilled in the base of its skull prior to the delivery of its head. It is this method that is colloquially known as "partial birth abortion".

Contrary to much of the publicity partial birth abortion has received it would appear to be no more painful to the foetus, and perhaps even less painful to the foetus than *in utero* dismemberment. It is also believed to be a safer procedure for the mother to undergo as it prevents the possibility of haemorrhage caused by broken foetal bones rupturing the uterine walls, or infection as the result of interuterine foetal bleeding. However, the least painful method of abortion for the foetus at this stage of development, as it was in the pre-24-week-old foetus, is via an intracardiac injection of potassium chloride. This method, as mentioned previously, is apparently rarely employed, and when it is employed it is employed in order to reduce emotional distress to the people involved in the process, rather than to reduce foetal suffering.

---

[15] Section 10 of the *Crimes Act* 1958 (Vic) states that "Any person who, with intent to destroy the life of a child capable of being born alive...causes such child to die...shall be guilty of child destruction". "Capable of being born alive" in this context is defined in s.10(2) as 28 weeks or more of pregnancy.

[16] See Victorian Government, *op.cit.*

How can such acts be justified? Is there any justification for the deliberate taking of a post-24-week-old foetus's life? Is there any justification for knowingly causing the post-24-week-old foetus pain and suffering? Many would perhaps answer "yes" to this question "a reduction of suffering by the mother, and the mother's right to control her own body", it could be argued, "are sufficient to justify such acts".

Practicalities and Mothers

The post-24-week-old foetus has, as we have seen, an interest in continued existence that is a result of its future desires. The mother, on the other hand, has an interest in continued existence that is a result of her past or presently experienced desires. Consequently, in cases in which only the foetus or the mother can survive, a choice between their conflicting interests must be made. In all other cases in which an innocent person's interest in continued existence is threatened, that person has a right to use as much force as is necessary to ensure his/her continued existence. The case at hand would appear to be no different; if the mother's life is threatened by the presence of the foetus she has a right to defend herself, even if her self-defence results in the death of the foetus.

But, it could be argued, the right to self-defence does not normally justify the use of force against an innocent party, and clearly the abortion of a post-24-week-old foetus would constitute such force. The special relationship between the mother and the foetus creates a unique situation however: namely, if the mother were to die as a result of the foetus's presence *in utero*, the foetus would also die *in utero*. Consequently, a threat to the mother's life by the foetus *in utero* is also a threat to the foetus's life *in utero*; such a threat consequently justifies the foetus's removal from the mother. In many cases in which the foetus is 24 weeks or older, its removal would not necessitate its death. But, even it were to do so, its removal would still be justified.

To say that the foetus's removal is justified, however, is not to say that the use of excessive force can be justified. If the foetus threatening the mother's life can be removed alive, the mother's right to self-defence only gives the mother a right to remove it from her body, it does not give her a right to kill it. Similarly, the right to self-defence does not provide a justification for the causing of unnecessary pain to the foetus. The mother's right to self-defence grants her only the right to save herself in such a way as to cause the minimum amount of harm and suffering to the foetus that is compatible with not inflicting too great a degree of pain on herself. That said, if the only way for the mother to defend herself is to abort the foetus, and in so doing she causes it to suffer or to die, she would be justified in doing so.

Some may perhaps argue in response to this that if the mother's right to self-defence can justify the removal and perhaps death of the foetus, would it not be the case that the foetus, as a being with an interest in continued existence, also has a right to self-defence which could justify the intervention of a third party on behalf of the foetus? It seems to me that as the pre-viable foetus is dependent on the mother for its survival, the presence of the mother could not constitute a threat to its continued existence; as such one could not justify an invasion of the mother's autonomy in order to remove the foetus.

The question becomes more difficult in the case of a viable foetus whose life is threatened by its remaining *in utero*. In many such cases, the threat to the foetus would also constitute a threat to the mother, and action will need to be taken in order to safeguard the mother's life. There may be a small minority of cases, however, in which the threat to the foetus's life by remaining *in utero* is immediate, whereas the threat to the mother will only eventuate if the foetus dies. Even in these cases however, it is hard to see how one could justify compelling the mother to undergo surgery to save the foetus, when the surgery itself may place the mother's life in danger. Added to this, issues concerning a mother's right to self-determination would further tip the balance in favour of upholding the mother's desires in such a situation.

Consequently, it is unlikely that a post-24-week-old foetus's right to self-defence could justify others acting so as to protect its interests whilst it is *in utero* against the wishes of the mother. The mother is justified in protecting herself against the foetus as an innocent party only because her death would result in the foetus's removal or death anyway. In which case, the foetus's removal, and/or death is an unavoidable consequence of the situation: if the mother's life is threatened by the presence of the foetus, and if the foetus is not removed and she dies, so too will the foetus. The only question to be asked in such a situation is therefore whether the mother ought to be allowed to save herself. Clearly, she should. But, the same is not true in reverse. Even if the foetus's life is threatened by its continued presence *in utero*, it would not necessarily be the case that were it not removed the mother would die anyway. The two situations are not therefore interchangeable.

In cases in which genuine medical emergencies arise and in which either the foetus or the mother must die, it is not simply a matter of choosing between two conflicting yet equal interests in continued existence. Every being with an interest in continued existence has a corresponding right to self-defence, the mother that is threatened by an unborn foetus can therefore justifiably use such force as is necessary in order to save herself if she is threatened. Even when such action is justified though, the mother's over-riding interest in survival would not justify unnecessary pain being caused to the foetus. The mother's interest in continuing to exist would not, in other words, grant her the right to cause the foetus a painful death if a painless one were available that did not impose too great a burden on her.

What is more, it would seem probable that in the vast majority of cases in which a woman had carried a pregnancy through to 24 weeks or more before discovering that it was necessary to terminate it in order to survive, she would be loathe to cause the unborn foetus any more suffering than was necessary to save herself. And, in many cases if these women were made aware of the greater pain and suffering caused by some abortion procedures over others, it is plausible to suppose that in a majority of cases they would opt for the least painful one to the foetus, even if it meant greater personal suffering to themselves. This possibility, whilst not empirically proven, would seem to follow from the claims that many involved with abortion make regarding the distress of the mother over the necessity of the procedure, and the questions often asked by the mothers in regards to the possibility of the foetus suffering.

The fact that this question is routinely answered in the negative also raises questions concerning the informed consent of the mother, and the likelihood of her being able to make an autonomous decision regarding the removal, and in many cases the ensuing death of the foetus when given such misinformation. If, as we have seen, there are procedures available that would avoid the prolonged suffering of the foetus that is the result of currently acceptable abortion procedures, many women if placed in such a position may well choose these procedures, especially given that such procedures do not significantly impact on the physical suffering of the mother, and may well positively decrease the emotional suffering of the mother. Not to be given the information necessary in order to do so is unacceptable.

It needs to be stressed however, that in all but genuine emergencies, abortion of a post-24-week-old foetus would not be a justifiable act. And, in the vast majority of emergencies the mother's right to self-defence would grant her only the right to remove the foetus, it would not grant her the right to kill it. The injunctions so far mentioned, however, are applicable only to the "normal" post-24-week-old human foetus that has an interest in continuing to exist as a consequence of its being the very same enduring subject of experience as the person it will one day become. There are some foetuses that do not fit this definition.

Practicalities and Abnormal Foetuses

Some foetuses are so badly deformed that they will never become persons. In these cases (of which anaecephalic foetuses are one example) there will never be a capacity to interact with the social world. Hence there can be no active potential to become a person, and no subject of experience that is psychologically connected and/or continuous with a person. Consequently, such foetuses cannot have an interest in continued existence, and aborting them is therefore not an intrinsically wrong act.

Whether or not such foetuses would have an interest in not being caused pain is a separate issue, and is dependent on the specific capacities of the foetus in question. It could, for instance, be the case that some foetuses are capable of experiencing pain even though they cannot interact with the world around them on a conscious level,[17] in which case they would have an interest in not being caused pain despite their defects. In cases in which the deformity of the foetus means there is no active potential for personhood and no capacity to experience pain, there are no moral restrictions as to the type of procedures employed to abort them. But, in cases in which the deformity of the foetus means that there is no active potential for personhood but in which there is a capacity to experience pain, acceptable abortion procedures ought be restricted to those discussed in the earlier section regarding the pre-24-week-old foetus that is sentient but not yet conscious.

---

[17] This is particularly likely if the claims that were discussed earlier regarding the possibility of foetal sentience prior to a functioning cortex are correct. See pages 82 – 86 above.

Another set of cases that requires mentioning is that which is comprised of foetuses with an active potential to become persons, that are the very same subject of experience as the person they would become, but which have disabilities so severe that their life would be filled with suffering (such as a foetus with very severe Spina Bifida). So long as a foetus has an active potential to become a person it has an interest in continued existence and aborting it would be *prima facie* wrong. Any justification for the deliberate killing of such a foetus would therefore have to rest on the same quality of life decisions as are employed in the active termination of actual persons' lives. That is to say that the justification for the death of such foetuses would fall within the euthanasia debate not the abortion debate.

One final set of cases that must be mentioned are those foetuses with an active potential to become persons, that are the very same subject of experience as the persons they will become, but which have a disability that will prevent their full participation in social life but not necessarily reduce their subjective quality of life: a foetus with mild Downs Syndrome would be such a case. In these cases the foetus has an interest in continued existence due to its psychological continuity with the person it will become. And, as the person the foetus will become is likely to have a reasonable quality of life, it is unlikely that killing it could be justified. In all other cases the post-24-week-old foetus, as we have seen, has an active potential to become a person, it is the very same enduring subject of experience as the person it becomes, and it has an interest in continued existence that can only be over-ridden by greater moral interests, such as the mother's interest in continued existence in some cases. Consequently, in all such cases abortion is *prima facie* wrong.

Practicalities and Non-Human Animals

Finally, it should be noted that none of what has been discussed in this chapter, in regards to our treatment of the human foetus, could consistently be restricted to human foetuses alone. There is currently a large and seemingly incoherent division drawn between human and non-human foetuses and animals. This division sanctions, on the one hand, the painful and prolonged death of human foetuses, yet demands the intentional avoidance of a prolonged or painful death being caused to non-human foetuses. On the other hand, it legally sanctions the killing of late term non-human foetuses (some of which may also possess an active potential to become a person), whilst simultaneously legislating, but not enforcing sanctions against the killing of late term human foetuses. Such a position is simply incoherent and untenable.

In all cases, human and non-human, it is the capacity or lack of the capacity to feel pain that grants a being an interest in not being caused pain, and the interest in continuing to exist that grants it a right to continue to exist. Consequently, it is *prima facie* wrong to cause pain to *any* being that has a capacity to feel pain, or to kill *any* being that has an interest in continuing to exist.[18] To draw boundaries across the application of these principles on the basis of species membership is unacceptable. If it is *prima facie* wrong to kill or cause pain to a human foetus that is a potential person, it is also *prima facie* wrong to kill or cause pain to any other foetus that is a potential person. In all cases only a very compelling reason, justified by the presence of greater interests that could justify such a violation of that interest, and even in the face of such reasons, only those interests that necessarily must be infringed in order to uphold the greater moral interest can justifiably be infringed.

---

[18] It could be asked in response to this claim, why the presence of a basic psychological continuity in most mammals and reptiles would not grant them a right to continue to exist too. This would be to misinterpret the earlier argument however. The importance of Relation R between the post-24-week-old foetus and the person it becomes is that it shows that the foetus with an active potential to become a person is the very same subject of experience as the person it develops into. Mere psychological continuity between two non-persons would itself have no moral significance. In order to have a right to continue to exist it is necessary, as was discussed earlier, for the foetus to have an active potential to become a person – which includes but is not limited to a genetic structure appropriate to the manifestation of personhood and a manifest capacity to interact with the social world; it must share at least a weak version of Parfit's Relation R with the person it becomes. Hence, the vast majority of non-human animals could never possess a right to continue to exist.

9 Conclusion

In order to address the issue of abortion this paper has predominantly focused on providing a response to Tooley's widely read discussion of the moral status of abortion and infanticide. In challenging Tooley no exception has been made to his understanding of actual persons, and the basis on which they have a right to continued existence. What has been challenged is his limiting of that right to actual persons only. It has been argued that the right to continue to exist ought to be extended to potential persons because they are the very same enduring subject of experience as the person they will become, and it can therefore plausibly be assumed that they will come to possess the corresponding desire if they are not interfered with. In making this claim though, support has not been provided for the anti-abortionist stance, which portrays the destruction of the human embryo and foetus as intrinsically and always morally problematic. Rather, it has been argued that in the case of human potential persons, only the post-24-week-old foetus has a right to continue to exist, because only the post-24-week-old foetus has an active potential to become a person. Consequently, it is only after this point in foetal development that abortion is *prima facie* wrong.

As a result of this argument three things have been determined. Firstly, it has been shown that invasive procedures, such as abortion, that are directed towards the pre-sentient human embryo are not morally problematic in themselves. The human embryo has no capacities that could cause it to suffer as a result of these procedures and hence no interest in not having such procedures carried out. Furthermore, the human embryo is not a subject of any experiences, and hence not psychologically connected or continuous with the person or potential person it could become. Consequently, it is not the type of being that will come to have an interest in continuing to exist in the future. Early abortion, IVF procedures, and embryo experimentation are therefore not intrinsically wrong acts (though it remains unclear whether they could be said to have such undesirable side effects that they ought to be prevented on consequentialist grounds).

Secondly, it is uncertain whether or not a pre-24-week-old foetus can experience pain. But, given that there are accepted ethical guidelines that make it mandatory to treat non-human foetuses as if they are capable of experiencing pain unless there is indisputable evidence to the contrary, and given that there is a considerable amount of evidence to suggest that the human foetus may experience pain long before 24 weeks of development, it has been argued that the pre-24-week-old human foetus ought to be treated as if it can feel pain. That is to say that until there is indisputable evidence to the contrary, pre-24 weeks old foetuses ought to be treated as if they are sentient and capable of experiencing pain, and thus as if there is an intrinsic wrongness associated with the causing of pain in such foetuses. Consequently, abortion procedures should be swift and as painless as is possible for a foetus at this stage of development.

Even though the causing of unnecessary pain is unjustifiable at this stage in a foetus's development, however, killing it is not an intrinsically wrong act. For, the pre-24-week-old foetus does not have an active potential to become a person and it is not psychologically connected or continuous with the person it will become. Hence it does not have an interest in continued existence.

Finally, it has been determined that the post-24-week-old foetus not only has a definite interest in not being caused pain, it also has an interest in continued existence. It has an active potential to become a person, and it shares a weak version of Relation R with the person it becomes. It is thus the very same enduring subject of experience as the person it becomes, and its future desire to continue to exist grants it an interest in continuing to exist in the present; thus making it *prima facie* wrong to kill it in the present. Abortion procedures after the 24th week of pregnancy are therefore *prima facie* wrong, and only the mother's right to defend herself could override the foetus's interest.

Furthermore, even if the mother's right to self-defence were to justify aborting the post-24-week-old foetus, it would neither justify the intentional taking of its life, or the causing of unnecessary pain to the foetus. There may be rare and extreme cases in which the only way to save the life of the mother is through one of the more painful (for the foetus) abortion procedures. But, in the vast majority of cases abortion procedures that are relatively painless for the foetus are available and ought to be employed whenever the foetus's removal is required to save the mother's life. The enforcement of such procedures would not significantly infringe upon a woman's right to control her own body. It would however, limit her ability to cause pain and suffering and/or bring about the death of the foetus if she continues her pregnancy for several months before seeking an abortion.

In practical terms, this would mean in the vast majority of cases either aborting the embryo/foetus early in the pregnancy, bringing about a relatively painless death of the pre-viable foetus through the administration of intracardiac potassium chloride prior to its abortion, or adopting a mode of delivery commensurate with the viable foetus's survival.

The implementation of those procedures that are based on the post-24-week-old foetus's interest in continued existence, would have little overall effect on the availability of abortion, as all but a small number are carried out well before this stage of pregnancy. The pre-and post-24-week-old foetus's right not to be caused pain or suffering, however, significantly affects the morality of currently accepted abortion procedures, and will in many cases demand a review of these practices.

These findings are incommensurate with Tooley's liberal position on abortion, which reflects a belief that abortion is justified at any stage of pregnancy. The argument presented here is also incompatible with the conservative position on abortion, which views abortion as an intrinsically wrong act throughout the entirety of a pregnancy. In contrast to both of these views, the moderate position developed within these pages focuses on the dynamic nature of the unborn human's development: as rapidly developing beings the human embryo and foetus cross the boundaries of mere biological existence, through mere sentience, to existence as potential persons with an interest in continued existence. As such, it is implausible to suggest that one unchanging ethical position can adequately account for our moral responsibilities towards them. It is for this reason that the argument presented in this paper has been aimed at providing an empirically grounded, justifiable and non-arbitrary philosophical basis for the treatment of unborn humans from the time they are conceived until the time they are born. And, this in the end is, or ought to be, the goal of medical ethics – to determine a philosophically sound and empirically practicable ethic to guide our treatment of others.

Bibliography

Anand, K.J.S. and Hickey, P.R. (1987) 'Pain and its effects in the human neonate and foetus', pp. 1321-1329 of *The New England Journal of Medicine*, v.317.

Belzer, Marvin (1996) 'Notes on Relation R', *Analysis* 56 (1), Jan.

Bergstrom, R.M. (1969) 'Electrical parameters of the brain during ontogeny', pp. 15-41 of Robinson, R.J. (ed) *Brain and Early Behaviour: Development in the Foetus and Infant*, Academic Press, London.

Bower, T.G.R. (1974) *Development in Infancy*, WH Freeman and Company, San Francisco.

Brokowski, W.J. and Berstine, R.L. (1955) 'Electroencephalography of foetus', pp. 362-365 of *Neurology* 5.

Buckle, Stephen (1990) 'Arguing from Potential', pp. 90-108 of Singer, P., Kuhse, H., Buckle, S., Dawson, K. and Kasimba, P. (eds.) *Embryo Experimentation*, Cambridge University Press, Cambridge.

Burgess, J.A. and Tawia, S.A. (1996) 'When did you first begin to feel it? – Locating the beginning of human consciousness', pp. 1-26 of *Bioethics*, v.10(1), Jan.

DeCasper, A.J. and Fifer, W.P. (1980) 'Of human bonding: newborns prefer their mother's voices', pp. 1174-1176 of *Science*, v.208.

DeCasper, A.J. and Spence, M.J. (1986) 'Prenatal maternal speech influences newborn's perception of speech sounds', pp. 133-150 of *Infant Behaviour and Development*, v.9.

Dehaene-Lambertz, G. and Denaene, S. (1994) 'Speed and cerebral correlates of syllable discrimination in infants', pp. 292-294 of *Nature*, v.37.

De Vries, J.I.P. Visser, G.H.A. and Prechtl, H.F.R. (1982) 'The emergence of foetal behaviour I: Qualitative aspects', pp. 301-322 of *Early Human Development* 7.

Eisenberg, Leon (1995) 'Social Construction of the Human Brain', pp. 1563-1569 of *American Journal of Psychiatry*, v.152 (11), Nov.

Feinberg, J. (1974) 'The Rights of Animals and Unborn Generations', pp. 43-68 of Blackstone, William T. (ed.) *Philosophy and Environmental Crisis*, Athens, Georgia.

Feinberg, J. (1980) 'Abortion', pp. 183-217 of Regan, T. (ed.) *Matters of Life and Death: New Introductory Essays in Moral Philosophy*, Random House Press, New York.

Field, Tiffany (1985) 'Neonatal perception of people and individual differences', pp. 31-52 of Field, Tiffany M. and Fox, Nathan A. (eds) *Social Perception in Infants*, Ablex Publishing Corporation, New Jersey.
Fifer, W.P. and Moon, C. (1989) 'Psychobiology of new-born auditory preferences', pp. 430-433 of *Seminars in Perinatology*, v.13.
Fitzgerald, M. (1995) *Foetal pain: an update of current scientific knowledge*, Department of Health, London.
Fivush, R. and Hammond, N.R. (1990) 'Autobiographical memory across the preschool years: Toward reconceptualising childhood amnesia', pp. 223-248 of Fivush, R. and Hudson, J. (eds) *Knowing and Remembering in Young Children*, Cambridge University Press, New York.
Franz, Wanda (1981) 'Foetal Development: A novel Application of Piaget's Theory of Cognitive Development', pp. 36-44 of Hilgers, T., Horan, Dennis J. and Mall, David (eds.) *New Perspectives on Human Abortion*, Aletheia Books, Maryland.
Gagnon, R. (1989) 'Stimulation of human foetuses with sound and vibration', pp. 393-402 of *Seminars in Perinatology*, v.13.
Giannakoulopoulos, X., Sepulveda, W., Kourtis, P., Glover, V., and Fisk, N.M. (1994) 'Foetal plasma cortisol and beta-endorphin response to intrauterine needling', pp. 77-81 of *The Lancet* 344.
Gilles, F.J., Shankle, W. and Dooling, E.C. (1983) pp. 117-183 of Gilles, F.J., Leviton, A., and Dooling, E.C. (eds) *The Developing Human Brain: Growth and Epidemiological Neuropathy*, John Wright, Boston.
Gillespie, Norman C. (1977) 'Abortion and Human Rights', pp. 237-243 of *Ethics*, v.87 (3).
Glover, Vivette and Fisk, Nicholas (1996) 'Commentary: We Don't know; better to err on the safe side from mid-gestation', p. 796 of *The British Medical Journal*, v.313, 28 September.
Goswami, Usha (1998) *Cognition in Children*, Psychology Press, London.
Hegel, G.W.F. (1954) 'The Phenomenology of Spirit', in Friedrich, Carl J. (ed.) *The Philosophy of Hegel*, Modern Library, New York.
Hepper, Peter G. (1989) 'Foetal Learning: Implications for Psychiatry', pp. 289-293 of *British Journal of Psychiatry'*, 155.
Hepper, Peter G. (1991) 'An examination of foetal learning before and after birth', pp. 95-107 of *Irish Journal of Psychology*, v.12 (2).
Hepper, Peter G. (1992) 'Foetal psychology: an embryonic science', in Nijhuis, J.G (ed.) *Foetal Behaviour: Developmental and Perinatal Aspects*, Oxford University Press, New York.

Hepper, Peter G. and Shahidullah, Sara (1994) 'The beginnings of mind – evidence from the behaviour of the foetus', pp. 143-154 of *Journal of Reproductive and Infant Psychology*, v.12.

House of Lords (1996) *The Problem of Pain: A Report by the Commission of Inquiry into Foetal Sentience'* at http://www.care.org.uk/issues/fs/hs05.htm, commissioned by the House of Lords, London.

Howe, M.L. and Courage, M.L. (1993) 'On resolving the enigma of infantile autism', pp. 305-326 of *Psychological Bulletin*, 113.

Humphrey, T. (1964) 'Some correlations between the appearance of human foetal reflexes and the development of the nervous system', pp. 93-135 of *Progress in Brain Research* 4.

Kay, Kenneth (1982) *The Mental and Social Life of Babies*, University of Chicago Press, Chicago.

Kinney, H.C. Korein, J. Panigraphy, A. Dikkes, P. and Goode, R. (1994) 'Neuropathological Findings in the Brain of Karen Ann Quinlan – The Role of the Thalamus in the Persistent Vegetative State', pp.1469-1475 of *The New England Journal of medicine*, v.330 (21), May.

Klaus, Marshall H. and Klaus, Phyllis (1985) *The Amazing Newborn*, Addison-Wesley Publishing, Massachusetts.

Kluge, Eike-Henner W. (1978) 'Infanticide as the Murder of Persons' pp. 32-45 of Kohl, Marvin (ed) *Infanticide and the Value of Life*, Prometheus Books, New York.

Kolata, Gina (1984) 'Studying learning in the womb', pp. 302-304 of *Science*, v.225, July 20.

Kozak Mayer, Nancy and Tronick, Edward Z. (1985) 'Mother's turn-giving signals and infant turn-taking in mother-infant interaction', pp. 199-216 of Field, Tiffany M. and Fox, Nathan A. (eds) *Social Perception in Infants*, Ablex Publishing Corporation, New Jersey.

Kuljis, R.O. (1994) 'Development of human brain: the emergence of the neural substrate for pain perception and conscious experience', pp. 49-56 of Bellar F.K. and Weir R.F. (eds) *The Beginnings of Human Life,* Kluwer Academic Publishers, The Netherlands.

Langerak, Edward (1979) 'Abortion: Listening to the Middle', pp. 24-28 of *Hastings Center Report*, v.9 (5), Oct.

Laroche, J.C. (1981) 'The marginal layer in the neocortex of a 7 week-old human embryo', pp. 301-312 of *Anatomy and Embryology* 162.

Liley, A.W. (1972) 'The foetus as a personality', pp. 99-105 of *Australian and New Zealand Journal of Psychiatry*, v.6.

Liley, Sir William (1981) 'A Day in the Life of the Foetus', pp. 29-35 of Hilgers, Thomas, Horan, Dennis J. and Mall, David (eds.) *New Perspectives on Human Abortion*, Aletheia Books, Maryland.

Lipsett, L.P. (1990) 'Learning processes in the human newborn', pp. 113-127 of *Annals of New York Academy of Sciences*, v.608.

Lloyd-Thomas, Adrian R. and Fitzgerald, Maria (1996) 'For Debate: Reflex Responses do not Necessarily Signify Pain', pp. 797-798 of *The British Medical Journal*, v.313, 28 September.

Lorber, J. (1965) 'Hydraencephaly with normal development', pp. 628-633 of *Developmental Medicine and Child Neurology*, v.7.

Mackie, J.L. (1975) 'Cause and Conditions', pp. 15-38 of Ernest Sosa (ed) *Causes and Conditionals*, Oxford University Press, London.

Marin-Padilla, M. (1978) 'Dual origin of the mammalian neocortex and evolution of the cortical plate', pp. 109-126 of *Anatomy and Embryology* 12.

Marin-Padilla, M. and Marin-Padilla, M.T. (1982) 'Origin, prenatal development and structural organisation of layer I of the human cerebral (motor) cortex', pp. 161-206 of *Anatomy and Embryology* 201.

McCullagh, P. (1996) 'Foetal Sentience: A paper published by the All-party parliamentary Pro-Life Group', *Catholic Medical Quarterly* XLVII, no.2, Nov.

Mehler, J. (1998) 'A precursor to language development in young infants', pp. 143-178 of *Cognition*, v.29.

Meltzoff, Andrew N. (1985) 'The Roots of Social and Cognitive Development: Models of Man's Original Nature', pp. 1-30 of Tiffany M. Field and Nathan A. Fox (ed) *Social Perception in Infants*, Ablex Publishing Corporation, New Jersey.

More, Max (1995) *The Diachronic Self: Identity, Continuity and Transformation*, http://www.primnet.com/~maxmore/chapter1.htm.

National Health and Medical Research Council (1997) *Australian Code of Practice for the Care and Use of Animals for Scientific Purposes*, Sep.

National Health and Medical Research Council (1998) *Draft Statement on Ethical Conduct in Research Involving Humans*, July.

Noonan, John T. (1981) 'The Experience of Pain by the Unborn', pp. 205-216 of Hilgers, Thomas., Horan, Dennis J. and Mall, David (eds.) *New Perspectives on Human Abortion*, Aletheia Books, Maryland.

Okado, N. (1980) 'Development of the human cervical spinal cord with reference to synapse formation in the motor nucleus', pp. 495-513 of *Journal of Comparative Neurology* 191.

Okado, N. (1981) 'Onset of synapse formation in the human spinal cord', pp. 211-219 of *Journal of Comparative Neurology* 201.

Pahel, Kenneth R. (1987) 'Michael Tooley on Abortion and Potentiality', pp.89-107 of *the Southern Journal of Philosophy*, v. XXV (1).

Parfit, Derek (1984) *Reasons and Persons*, Clarendon Press, Oxford.

Peleg, D. and Goldman, J.A. (1980) 'Foetal heart rate acceleration in response to light stimulation as a clinical measure of foetal well-being: a preliminary report', pp. 38-41 of *Journal of Perinatal Medicine* v.8.

Piontelli, Alessandra (1992) *From Foetus to Child: an observational and psychoanalytic study*, Routledge, London.

Ranalli, Paul (1998) *Abortion and the Unborn Baby: The Painful Truth*, at http://www.california.prolife/paintrut.htm

Royal College of Obstetricians and Gynaecologists (1997) *Foetal Awareness: report of a working party*, RCOG Press, London.

Sallanbach, William B. (1994) 'Claira: A Case Study in Prenatal Learning', pp. 33-56 of *Pre- and Perinatal Psychology Journal*, 9(1), Fall.

Schaal, B. and Orgeur, P. (1992) 'Olfaction *in utero*, Can the rodent model be generalised', pp. 245-278 of *Quarterly Journal of Experimental Psychology*, v.44B.

Shahidullah, S. and Hepper, P.G. (1993) 'The developmental origins of foetal responsiveness to an acoustic stimulus', pp. 135-142 of *Journal of Reproductive and Infant Psychology*, v.11.

Singer, Peter (1980) 'Animals and the Value of Life', pp. 218-259 of T. Regan (ed.) *Matters of Life and Death: New Introductory Essays in Moral Philosophy*, Random House Press, New York.

Singer, Peter (1986) *Applied Ethics*, Oxford University Press, New York.

Singer, Peter (1993) *Practical Ethics* (2nd ed.) Cambridge University Press, Cambridge.

Stone, Jim (1987) 'Why Potentiality Matters', pp. 815-830 of *Canadian Journal of Philosophy*, v.17, no.4, Dec.

Sumner, L.W. (1974) 'Toward a Credible View of Abortion', pp. 163-181 of *Canadian Journal of Philosophy*, v. IV (1), Sept.

Thompson, J.J. (1971) 'A Defence of Abortion', pp. 47-66 of *Philosophy and Public Affairs*, 1(1).

Tooley, Michael (1983) *Abortion and Infanticide*, Clarendon Press, Oxford.

Tooley, Michael (1987) *Causation: a realist approach*, Oxford University Press, Oxford.

Victorian Government (1998) *Victorian Government Report on late term terminations of pregnancy*, April, found at http://hna.ffh.vic.gov.au/abs/report

Vintner, A. (1986) 'The role of movement in eliciting early imitations', pp. 66-71 of *Child Development*, 57.

Index

Abortion, 1, 2, 5, 24, 37, 60, 90-92, 100-107
   conservative theory, 1, 101
   feminist theory, 1
   liberal theory, 1, 101
   moderate theory, 1, 101
Abortion Practices, 87, 90, 95, 96, 100
   Australia, 90, 92
   dilation and curettage, 90
   injection of prostaglandin, 90, 92
   intracardiac injection of potassium chloride, 91, 92, 101
   partial birth abortion, 90, 92
   suction curettage, 90
Acts and omissions, 79
Anaesthesia, 87-89
Analgesics, 29, 30
Anand, K.J.S., 103
Asymmetry, 73, 76, 77
Background causal field, 9, 11, 13, 14, 15, 20, 68, 83
Belzer, Marvin, 48, 55, 103
Bergstrom, R.M., 26, 103
Berstine, R.L., 25, 103
Blackstone, W.T., 64, 103
Bower, T.G.R., 42, 44, 103
Brain, 20, 21, 24, 25, 27, 31, 32, 46, 69, 87, 92, 103, 104, 105
   cortex, 24-31, 46, 87, 96, 106
   motor system, 37
   myelination, 26
   neural pathways, 21
   pain receptors, 28, 52
   sense receptors, 28, 30, 32, 36
   spino-thalamic system, 23, 27
   stem, 25, 31
   thalamus, 25, 26, 27, 28, 29, 31, 32, 87, 105
Brokowski, W.J., 25, 103
Buckle, S.,
   potential to become, 2, 3, 4, 7, 11, 12-17, 22, 33, 39, 45, 46, 59, 60, 61, 63, 66, 68, 70, 71, 76, 77, 78, 80, 83, 84, 85, 91, 96-100
   potential to produce, 7, 11, 76
Burden of proof, 87, 89
Burgess, J.A., 19, 20, 27, 28, 103
Casual fields, 9
Causal factors of personhood, 3, 7-17, 19, 22, 33, 45, 46, 59, 62, 68, 83, 84
   arbitrary, 1, 9, 14, 83
   external, 3, 8, 9, 12, 20, 68, 83
   internal, 9
Causal processes, 60, 73, 74, 75, 76, 80
Cognition, 31, 38, 40, 41, 104, 106
Cognitive abilities of the foetus, 35, 37, 104, 106
Cognitive processes, 56, 57
Consciousness, 19, 22-32, 35, 36, 38, 45, 46, 53, 58, 59, 67, 69, 70, 84, 88, 103
Courage, M.L, 57, 105
Crimes Act 1958 (Vic), 92
De Vries, J.I.P., 25, 26, 103
DeCasper, AJ., 39, 40, 41, 43, 51, 103
Dehaene-Lambertz, G., 40, 51, 103
Denaene, S., 40, 51, 103
Development

foetal, 1, 27, 52, 53, 84, 88, 99
  physiological, 3, 9, 13, 16, 18, 23, 25, 28, 29, 30, 45, 53, 61, 76
  psychological, 2, 3, 4, 14, 15, 17, 20-24, 27, 28, 30, 35, 37, 41, 44-53, 55-61, 63-66, 68, 70, 76, 77, 84, 88, 97, 98, 105
  social, 19-24, 30, 33-46, 50, 55, 59, 62, 84, 96, 97, 98, 103-106
Dikkes, P., 105
Dooling, E.C., 104
Downs Syndrome, 97
Eisenberg, L., 20, 21, 40, 103
Embryo, 4, 7, 22, 58, 61, 62, 78, 83, 85, 86, 88, 99, 101, 103, 105
Embryo experimentation, 5, 7, 83, 86, 99, 103
Feinberg, J., 64, 70, 103
Field, T., 34, 35, 43, 44, 45, 104, 105, 106
Fifer, W.P., 39, 40, 41, 103, 104
Fisk, N., 27, 29, 33, 104
Fitzgerald, M., 24, 26, 27, 28, 29, 30, 52, 53, 104, 106
Fivush, R., 57, 104
Foetal emotions, 27, 28, 29
Foetal learning, 31, 37, 38, 39, 40, 41, 45, 56, 104, 105
Foetal pain, 24, 25, 26, 27, 31, 34, 87, 88, 89, 90, 96, 98, 100, 103, 105, 106
Foetal sentience, 22, 24-34, 45, 53, 59, 87-89, 96, 101, 105, 106
Foetal stress responses, 26, 29, 88
Foetus, as a subject, 4, 46, 58, 59, 62, 66, 76, 77, 85
Foetuses, abnormal, 96
Fox, N.A., 34, 43, 44, 104, 105, 106
Frankenstein, 69, 70
Franz, W., 37, 104

Gagnon, R., 35, 104
Genetic Structure, 20, 21
Genetic structure of foetus, 19-23, 33, 45, 59, 62, 84, 98
Giannakouloupoulos, X., 88, 104
Gilles, F.J., 26, 104
Gillespie, N.C., 104
Glover, V., 26, 27, 29, 33, 104
Goldman, J.A., 36, 107
Goode, R., 105
Habituation, 38, 39
Hammond, N.R., 57, 104
Hegel G.W.F., 20, 21, 104
Hepper, P.G., 27, 34, 35, 36, 37, 38, 39, 40, 42, 51, 52, 88, 104, 105, 107
Hickey, P.R., 88, 103
Hilgers, T., 24, 27, 37, 104, 106
Horan, D.J., 104, 106
Howe, M.L, 57, 105
Hudson, J., 57, 104
Humphrey, T., 26, 105
Hydraencephaly, 31, 106
Identity, 47, 49, 106
  numerical, 10, 11, 46, 47, 62, 85
  R relation, 3, 48-51, 55, 56, 58, 59, 62, 68, 71, 77, 84, 98, 100, 103
Individuation, 1
Infantile amnesia, 56, 57
Infantile autism, 57, 105
Infants
  anencephalic, 31
  hydracephalic, 31
Informed consent, 95
Interest in continued existence, 1, 2, 4, 5, 23, 63, 65, 67, 69-71, 77, 79, 80, 84-86, 90, 92-101
IVF Procedures, 5, 83, 86, 99
Kay, K., 34, 105
Kinney, H.C., 31, 105
Klaus, M.H., and P., 105

Klaus, M.H., 105
Kluge, E.H.W., 105
Kohl, M., 105
Kolata, Gina, 40, 51, 105
Korein, J., 105
Kourtis, P., 104
Kozak Mayer, N., 44, 105
Kuhse, H., 103
Kuljis, R.O., 25, 105
Langerak, E., 105
Language, 22, 40, 43, 106
Laroche, J.C., 26, 105
Learning, 39, 51, 52, 104, 106, 107
  associative, 31
  classical conditioning, 31, 38, 39
  discrimination, 43
  habituation, 38, 39, 40
  imitation, 42, 43, 44
  interactional synchrony, 42-44
  lower animals, 40
  memory, 29, 38, 39, 40, 41, 44, 46, 49, 52, 56, 57, 104
  theory, 8, 45, 47
  turn-taking, 42, 43, 44, 105
Liley, Sir W., 27, 30, 36, 52, 105, 106
Lipsett, L.P., 38, 106
Lloyd-Thomas, A.R., 24, 27, 28, 106
Lorber, J., 31, 106
Mackie, J.L., 8, 9, 106
Mall, D., 104, 106
Marin-Padilla, M., 25, 106
McCullagh, P., 25, 106
Mehler, J., 40, 51, 106
Meltzoff, A., 35, 106
Memories and Identity, 49, 56
Memory, 29, 38, 39, 40, 41, 44, 46, 49-52, 56, 57, 104
Moon, C., 39, 104
More, M., 2, 40, 46, 47, 49, 50, 68, 106

Mother-Infant Interaction, 22, 40, 43, 44, 105, 106
  imitation, 42, 43, 44
  interactional synchrony, 42-44
  turn-taking, 42, 44, 105
National Health and Medical Research Council (NH&MRC), 87, 88, 89, 90
Neonatal memory, 52
Non-human animals, 29, 30, 42, 83, 85, 87, 89, 91, 97, 98, 99
Non-momentary interests, 85
Noonan, J., 24, 27, 28, 30, 90, 106
Okado, N., 25, 106
Orgeur, P., 107
Pahel, K., 60, 64, 65, 66, 67, 76, 107
Pain, 23-34, 52, 63, 86-106
  House of Lords Report, 25, 105
  instantaneous, 28
  neurotransmitters, 88
  pathological, 28, 31
  physiological, 3, 9, 13, 16, 18, 23, 25, 28, 29, 30, 45, 53, 61, 76
  sensational, 28
Panigraphy, A., 105
Parfit, D., 3, 11, 47, 48, 49, 50, 51, 59, 61, 62, 84, 98, 107
  Relation R, 3, 48, 49, 50, 55, 56, 58, 59, 62, 68, 71, 77, 84, 98, 100, 103
Particular Interests Principle, 63, 64
Peleg, D., 36, 107
Personal identity, 3, 11, 47, 48, 59
Personhood, 2, 3, 8, 9, 11, 12, 14-17, 19-23, 33, 39, 45, 46, 48, 58, 59, 62, 68, 69, 70, 83, 84, 96, 98
  manifestation of, 8, 16, 18, 19, 22, 23, 45, 70, 98
  potential for, 2, 3, 7, 10, 14, 22, 23, 39, 68, 69, 70, 96
Persons

actual, 2, 3, 4, 11, 12, 15, 16, 20, 22, 23, 32, 34, 35, 47, 48, 49, 58, 59, 61, 66, 68, 69, 70, 74, 76, 84, 97, 99
possible, 4, 22, 24, 26, 30, 32, 37, 41, 54-58, 60, 64, 73-80, 83, 85, 86, 91, 100
Physical continuity, 85
Piaget, 37, 42, 45, 104
Piontelli, A., 53, 54, 55, 107
Positive causal factor, 3, 7-20, 22, 33, 45, 46, 59, 62, 68, 83, 84
Post-24-week-old foetus, 3, 4, 5, 30, 33, 34, 47, 48, 50, 52, 53, 55, 56, 58, 59, 61, 62, 68, 69, 71, 73, 78, 80, 84, 85, 91, 92, 93, 94, 96, 97, 98, 99, 100, 101
Potential, 7, 12, 19, 33, 45, 63, 103
active, 2, 3, 4, 7, 9-19, 22, 23, 33, 39, 42, 45, 46, 54, 59, 60, 61, 63, 66-71, 76, 77, 78, 80, 81, 83, 84, 85, 87, 91, 96, 97, 98, 99, 100
latent, 3, 7, 10, 11, 22, 70, 76, 80
passive, 7, 10, 12, 13, 35, 46, 54, 76, 77, 79
Potentiality Principle, 59, 60, 61, 75
Prechtl, H.F.R., 103
Pre-natal consciousness, 27, 32, 35, 36, 38
Principle of Moral Symmetry, 4, 73, 74, 75, 76, 77, 80, 81
Psychological awareness, 22, 45, 46, 53, 84
Psychological connectedness, 48, 49, 50, 51, 53, 55, 56, 57, 58, 68, 84
Psychological continuity, 48, 49, 50, 51, 53, 55, 56, 57, 58, 84, 85, 97, 98
Psychological states, 2, 14, 17, 50, 63, 65, 70

Qualitative studies of the foetus, 53, 55
Quality of life, 86, 97
Quickening, 1
Quinlan, Karen Ann, 31, 105
Radical egocentric, 35
Ranalli, P., 107
Regan, T., 103, 107
Right to continued existence, 1, 2, 4, 12, 33, 63, 64, 66, 68, 70, 73, 99
Right to self-defence, 93, 94, 95, 96, 100
Royal College of Obstetrcians and Gynaecologists (RCOG), 27, 107
Sallanbach, W.B., 51, 53, 107
Schaal, B., 107
Self-awareness, 1, 19, 20, 21, 23, 69
Self-defence, 93, 94, 95, 96, 100
Self-determination, women's, 94
Sensory experience
auditory, 35, 39, 40, 43, 104
chemosensory, 35, 36
touch, 24, 28, 32, 34, 35, 36, 89
visual, 35, 36, 43
Sentience, 22-28, 30-37, 44, 45, 47, 52, 53, 59, 63, 64, 76, 84, 87-89, 91, 96, 100, 101, 105, 106
Sepulveda, W., 104
Shahidullah, S., 35
Shankle, W., 104
Singer, P., 1, 2, 7, 87, 103, 107
Social Construction, 20, 103
Social context, 20
Social interaction, 19, 20, 21, 22, 23, 30, 33, 34, 35, 36, 38, 39, 42, 44, 45, 46, 50, 59, 62, 84, 96
social world, 19, 20, 21, 22, 23, 30, 33, 35, 36, 39, 42, 44, 45, 46, 50, 59, 62, 84, 96, 98
Spence, M.J., 39, 43, 51, 103

Spina Bifida, 97
Stone, J., 107
Subject of experiences, 4, 21, 46, 48, 51, 56, 58, 59, 62, 66, 76, 77, 84, 85, 91, 96, 97, 98, 99, 100
Sumner, L.W., 107
Tawia, S.A., 19, 20, 27, 28, 29, 103
The Cat in the Hat, 40
Thompson, J.J., 1, 107

Tooley, Michael, 2, 3, 4, 7-14, 17, 20, 59-70, 73-80, 83, 84, 85, 99, 101, 107
Tooley's kittens, 77
Tronick, E.Z., 43, 44, 105
Twins, 53, 54
Viability, 1
Vintner, A., 42, 43, 107
Visser, G.H.A., 103